EATING ALIVE

Prevention Thru Good Digestion

by Dr. Jonn Matsen N.D.

"The doctor of the future will give no medicine but
will interest his patients in the care of the human
frame, in proper diet, and in the cause and prevention
of disease."

Thomas A. Edison

140 recipes by Jeanne Marie Martin
Illustrations by Nelson Dewey

Crompton Books

Published by:

Canadian Address:
Crompton Books, Ltd.
156 West 3rd Street
North Vancouver, B.C.
Canada V7M 1E8
Tel: (604) 986-0987
Fax: (604) 986-3926

U.S. Address:
Crompton Books, Ltd.
943 Boblett Street
Blaine, WA
98230

Canadian Editions: 1987, 1988, 1989, 1990.
First American Edition, 1991.

Canadian Cataloguing in Publication Data
Matsen, Jonn, 1949-
EATING ALIVE: PREVENTION THRU GOOD DIGESTION

Includes index.
ISBN 0-9693586-0-1
1. Diet in disease   2. Digestion.
3. Diseases — Causes and theories of causation.   I. Title
RM216.M38 1988   615.8′54   C88-091437-8

Printed in the United States of America

This book is dedicated to Dr. Joe Boucher
whose strong shoulders and gentle heart helped
carry Naturopathy through some of its hardest years.

"The doctor of the future will give no medicine but will interest his patients in the care of the human frame, in proper diet, and in the cause and prevention of disease."

Thomas A. Edison

CONTENTS

PART II-EATING ALIVE

PART III - MENU PLANS AND RECIPES

"The physician who can cure one disease by a knowledge
of its principles may by the same means cure all the
diseases of the human body; for their causes are the same

Benjamin Rush, Physician

Signer of the Declaration
of Independence

INTRODUCTION

There is an incredible healing power within each of us that knows exactly what and where each of our ailments is and knows exactly what to do to correct them. That healing power is available to you at little cost and in unlimited quantities. It is, unfortunately, often stifled and dormant.

To activate this potential power all you need is to learn a little about how the body works and then follow through with a few simple steps.

Healing begins immediately. Within one week there is usually noticeable improvement. In three weeks many people feel better than they can ever remember. Deeper physical healing may take three months or more.

This book is intended for those who are healthy and want to stay that way, for those who are told they are healthy by conventional medical standards but who suspect otherwise, for those whose allergies haven't responded to shots, whose weight still hasn't come off, whose skin is still poor in spite of all the creams and ointments and lotions, and for those whose energy is so low that it seems they must be stuck in first gear.

It is for those whose menstrual cycles are full of cramps and bloating and wild mood swings which they still think are normal, for those whose digestion sputters and coughs like a car in need of a tune-up, for those who haven't become better from all the other diets, for those who've actually gotten worse from other diets, and most importantly for those who will one day have children, because a few months spent in improving health now will pay dividends for generations to come.

We've all known apparently innocent people who've been "struck down" by disease in the prime of life. Perhaps they were spiritually minded, athletic, have "eaten well" for years, never drank or smoked, loved and were loved by their families and enjoyed their jobs, yet still fell victim to an insidious disease. Disease looms as a deep dark ugly mystery in the face of this seeming injustice. Why should they, of all people, fall victim to disease? By the end of this book there will be little mystery left to disease. You will understand

what disease is and how to activate your body's suppressed desire to NOT have disease. Disease is truly weakened by the light of applied understanding.

It is so simple to prevent or even reverse most of those little nagging health problems that you will be amazed that a multi-billion dollar health care system has been built up that often is powerless to help and in some cases makes problems worse.

The examples of the healing process in action as shown later in letters from patients are true. The material in the book will not be "true" per se, however. The reason is that the explanations given are in terms of physiology. Human physiology is an inexact science and future insights into health and disease will prove some of the explanations to be incomplete. This will make little difference to the success of the program as the unpatentable healing medicine within us will not change even as future insights expand the knowledge of the human body.

This book is literally the best "story" that could be put together at this time to explain the improvements in health seen every day in my practise. It could be explained in a great deal more biochemical detail but I decided to emphasis concept rather than data. For those with a scientific mind and the need to know every little biochemical nuance I would suggest they subscribe to "A Textbook of Natural Medicine". This is an major ongoing project by the John Bastyr College of Naturopathic Medicine in Seattle to document in minute detail the biochemistry of Naturopathic Medicine.

While some of these testimonials are more dramatic than for the average patient, they are nonetheless typical. They are dramatic because the problems were considered irreversible and the agony of no hope can be more excruciating than the physical complaints. They are typical in that in spite of the wide variety of disease signs and symptoms, little or nothing was done for their specific complaints. Nothing was applied to the skin of the eczema patient, nothing was done for the hair of the girl with alopcia totalis, nothing was done for the thyroid of the lady with Hashimoto's. The testimonials could easily be expanded to include asthma, arthritis, acne, weak immunity, phobias, hypoglycemia, allergies, sinusitis, chronic indigestion, PMS, irregular menses, headaches, psoriasis, colitis etc.

All of these problems and more I have seen reversed without doing anything for the specific complaint. This doesn't mean that naturopathic medicine doesn't have local treatments or that local treatment should not be given. Neither is the case. It's just that when you activate the internal healing power the results can sometimes be so quick that the problem is healed from within before local treatment would be of any benefit.

Some patients have such weakened vitality that a doctor's skill will be tested to the limit and perhaps beyond. In these cases cooperation between the different health professions is important, to maximize the chances for return to health.

Some patients with major chronic problems may not experience improvement. It is imperative that anyone with a major problem be guided by a knowledgeable physician, as numerous hurdles to cure can present themselves.

Eating Alive will not solve all of your life problems, but if it leaves you with a little more understanding of the majesty of your body and a little less fear of disease, then it will have fullfilled its purpose.

If you use the information within wisely, you will enhance the innate desire of your body to prevent disease or possibly even to reverse it. Drugs and surgery are important and sometimes irreplaceable components of the conventional arsenal in the battle against disease. However, you will soon learn how to activate the more subtle but sometimes more effective healing force within you.

Dr. Jonn Matsen
North Vancouver, B.C.

PATIENTS' LETTERS

Hi, I'm a registered nurse. I was diagnosed as having mild osteo-arthritis of the left hip in the mid 1970's. The pain radiated from my lower back and hip up my whole spine. I was told that stress and coffee were causing this pain so I tried to overcome both these "causes".

I continued to get worse and was finally diagnosed as having ankylosing spondylitis which, if untreated, can become a crippling, deforming arthritis of the spine. In spite of therapy, I continued to need stronger anti-inflammatory drugs, to which I was allergic.

I did not wish to continue being dependent on medication so began trying natural forms of treatment. I stopped all the medication and tried to live with the pain and discomfort. The pain would become so severe that I would be forced to resort to medication for relief.

As I continued to seek natural source relief, I was introduced to Dr. Jonn Matsen, who tested me for food sensitivities, guided me through a cleansing period, hydrotherapy, food elimination and proper food combining. This was followed by an anti-fungus product containing caprylic acid.

Within the first two to three weeks of this program, I began to feel better physically and mentally, and became pain-free. An added bonus was the loss of weight. I have not resorted to medication since then.

Jean M. Empey R.N.
Vancouver, B.C.

I have scoliosis which resulted in muscle spasms in my back and neck and headaches. My chiropractor recommended that in conjunction with his treatments I consult Dr. Matsen regarding my nutritional status.

I would have thought of myself as already in good health as I am a registered nurse and run five miles a day, but I followed his instructions. There is much to be said for the success of this regime. I feel good! My energy level is much greater and my thought processes are much clearer. My back and neck tension is much less and I rarely have headaches.

Muriel Shaw R.N.

PART I

EATING TO DEATH:

Aspects of Anatomy, Physiology and Pathology in a NutShell

An Adventurous Journey Through Our Digestive System to Explore
the Mysterious Causes of Disease

"All the rules of prudence or gifts of experience
that life can accumulate will never do as much for
human comfort and welfare as would be done by a stricter
attention and a wiser science directed to the digestive
system."
Thomas DeQuincy 1785-1876

CHAPTER 1

The Stomach

Our poor digestive systems! From morning till night, from childhood to death, we put into our mouths more or less whatever we feel like having, whenever we feel like it. Whatever is within arm's reach may be consumed: Foods, liquids, stimulants, relaxants, chemicals, drugs. Anything and everything goes down the old hatch at some point in our lives.

We expect our system to somehow magically grind it all up, sort it out, use the good, eliminate the bad, all without any noise or complaint, and still leave us lots of energy. That the human system can withstand the abuse it does has to be one of the miracles of life. In fact, treating the digestive system like a garburetor may be harmful to your health.

The apparent stamina of the digestive system is illusory. From one to two years of age virtually everyone's stomach is in a state of "shock". Of over five thousand patients whom I've seen, only four people's stomachs showed adequate vitality. When the situation gets worse, it is called a hiatus hernia. Some doctors believe that over fifty per cent of the population over fifty has some degree of hiatus hernia. I would say that over 90% of the population has an early stage hiatus hernia starting by age three, though it may not show on an X-ray for many decades.

To get an idea of how we treat our stomach let's sit down and write a list of everything that we've put into our stomach in our life. Good Luck.

To begin digestion we first chew up food into swallowable portions. If we chew carbohydrates long enough, some will be completely digested by the alkaline digestive juices right in the mouth.

On swallowing, the food passes through a long tube called the esophagus (which penetrates a flat breathing muscle called the diaphragm) into the stomach. A fold of tissue functions as a valve to prevent the food and digestive juice from going back up the esophagus. The stomach has many layers of heavy muscle which make the stomach "churn" like a washing machine. As the stomach churns, it begins making acid digestive juices that digest protein, and mucous which protects the stomach from its own acid.

When the stomach is shown on an X-ray to have pulled up through the diaphragm so that part of it is now in the chest cavity, the patient has a hiatus hernia. It is a mystery to some doctors as to why this should be so common. Some blame a genetically short esophagus, but it's hard to imagine 50% of the population having a genetic problem. Obviously the diaphragm had a weakness that allowed the stomach to pull up through it.

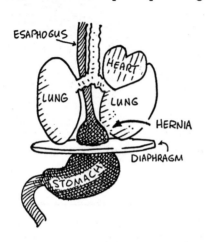

When the stomach is in a state of shock, this may slowly develop into an actual spasm of the stomach muscles. Spasm results in shortening of the muscle. In the more severe states even the muscles of the esophagus can spasm, causing it to shorten. Combine this shortened esophagus with a weakened diaphragm and you have a hiatus hernia. The irritation of the stomach begins early in childhood, even though the physical signs may not show on an X-ray till years later.

STOMACH TROUBLE IS THE BEGINNING OF DISEASE

Those little tummy aches as a child were the first signs of what might result in a chronic malfunction of the entire digestion system. The malfunctioning digestive system may result in almost every disease known to mankind.

Watch a baby. If there is something that doesn't agree with its stomach, the stomach quickly contracts, squeezing the irritant out one end or the other. Vomiting and diarrhea are two of the body's acute reactions to get rid of unwanted substances, to maintain homeostasis.

If the stomach which is continually exposed to irritation were to keep vomiting and having diarrhea, the health of the whole body would be put into jeopardy, so the stomach becomes "hardened". It still reacts to abuse by going into a state of shock, but no longer follows through with complete contraction to the point of actual vomiting and diarrhea. When that is the case we have established one-way communication with the stomach. We eat something and tell the stomach to take it and shut up, so the stomach stops telling us what it feels. This is the way we have gone through life. Thus is the soil readied for many a disease to germinate in.

The stomach is a pretty conscientious character. If we push it past its "hardened" state it will react. Nausea, vomiting, diarrhea, heart burn, indigestion, belching, gas, bloating, appetite disorders, and

ulcers are some of the signals that the stomach is having trouble. Rather than stop irritating the stomach so that it will go back to working properly, we often shut the stomach up even more. The biggest-selling drug in the world is Tagamet (cimetadine), which blocks histamine production by the stomach. Histamine is a chemical produced by tissue to aid inflammation, which is the body's natural reaction to irritation. Thus Tagamet effectively blocks the stomach's natural reaction to irritation. But does it stop the irritation?

The quantities of antacids, digestive aids and laxatives sold by pharmacies, health food stores and pyramid systems staggers the imagination. Everything from powerful drugs to foul-tasting herbal concoctions is sold. You would think that there wasn't a stomach left that worked properly. And you would be closer to the truth than you might suspect.

Some people get very severe and dramatic digestive symptoms when they eat, and it's not hard to convince them that abuse of the stomach is the cause of their problems. There are other patients, who eat with abandon and believe that their digestive systems are like garbage cans. "I can eat anything and everything," they say. If they have arthritis, heart attacks, skin problems, allergies, men-

strual problems, impotency or cancer, they don't correlate those problems with their diet or digestion, because they don't have the obvious digestive symptoms. They do have shocked stomachs however. Stomach malfunction is the cause of the other symptoms as well, even though they may appear to be unrelated.

ASSIMILATING MINERALS AND PROTEIN

There are several ways that stomach malfunction can cause problems far distant. If the stomach doesn't churn properly then a person won't make enough digestive juice. If there's not enough digestive juice, the nutrients won't be absorbed as well as they should. Stomach acid is important for the absorbtion of minerals and amino acids.

Calcium and iron have a positive charge and so does the lining of the intestinal tract. Like repels like, so the minerals tend to pass through the digestive system without being absorbed. If the stomach makes enough acid, the minerals pick up an extra positive charge from the acid, which then allows the mineral to bind with a protein. This protein is readily absorbed and it drags the mineral through with it. This is called chelation.

Mineral deficiencies are common in patients. Lack of stomach acid is one of the main causes of poor absorption of minerals. Though minerals are often not found in adequate amounts in processed-food diets, improving the diet will be of little benefit if the stomach doesn't also improve in function.

Proteins are long chains of amino acids coupled together like freight trains. There are more than twenty different types of amino acids, and the different sequences that they're arranged in determines what type of protein will be made. These protein "trains" have to be uncoupled so that the individual amino acid "cars" can be absorbed properly. It's the stomach acid that begins the breaking down of the proteins, so obviously poor stomach function could lead to amino acid deficiency, though this is relatively rare.

Poor protein digestion can also lead to "chunks" of amino acids still coupled together getting absorbed farther down in the intestinal tract. This can be an important factor in allergies.

Stomach acid is one of the natural antibiotics. Stomach acidity should be strong enough to kill most organisms in food.

Undersecretion of stomach juices can actually cause ulcers. If the stomach doesn't make enough mucous to protect itself from acid, even the slightest amount of acid can result in acid irritation, which can cause ulceration.

Stomach juice is also the "spark" that ignites the action of the intestine. The rhythmic contraction that is set into motion by stomach acid is called peristalsis. Poor stomach function can be one of the causes of constipation, as lack of acid stimulation can result in decreased peristalsis. You know that a car with fouled-up spark plugs can't run smoothly, and neither can the intestine with a fouled stomach.

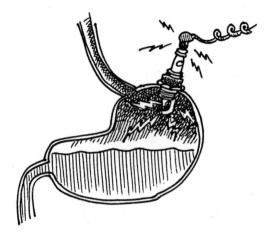

So we can see that the stomach is extremely important for absorption of nutrients, especially of the building materials: amino acids and minerals. The stomach is also an important defense organ and provides the spark for the rest of the digestive system. It's no wonder that the stomach is found in the center of the body or solar plexus, as it is truly the center of our physical universe.

Yet we've already talked about the stomach as malfunctioning in virtually everyone since early childhood. How could people continue to live in apparent health? Wouldn't medical doctors have discovered this?

The following is a quote from a book on the digestive system written by Eugene S. Jacobson, M.D.:

"The stomach is important to our lives in three main ways: first, it stores food and fluids temporarily, allowing us to eat large meals; second, it secretes the intrinsic factor without which a fatal pernicious anemia may develop; and third, the organ is involved in peptic ulcers, gastric carcinoma and gastritis, bleeding and indigestion. Because of the frequency of these latter disorders, the subject of gastric secretion is of enormous interest. Gastric secretions are also involved in the digestion of food and in bacteriostasis, but such actions of the stomach are not as critical contributions to the body."

This paragraph pretty much sums up the neglect that medicine has given to our poor abused stomach. We might just as well remove this sickly thing surgically and replace it with a garbage bag.

PANCREAS TO THE RESCUE

After the stomach has hopefully churned away and its digestive juices have worked over the mass of food, the food finally passes through the pyloric valve and into the duodenum, which is the beginning of the intestinal tract. The duodenum is about ten inches long. A small duct enters it just below the stomach. This duct brings alkaline bile from the liver and gallbladder to help emulsify fats and lubricate the intestine, and also large quantities of alkaline enzymes from the pancreas. These digestive enzymes from the pancreas can digest carbohydrates, proteins and fats.

The pancreas is thus the cleanup hitter of the digestive system. What the mouth and the stomach have failed to digest, the pancreatic enzymes will readily finish. It is this group of digestive enzymes that most of us are relying on for the bulk of our digestion, as the stomach is not contributing as much as it should. Not chewing carbohydrates thoroughly puts even greater stress on the pancreas.

Digestion can, then, go on reasonably well without proper stomach function, due to the pancreas doing most of the work. However, to stimulate the pancreas and gallbladder to work properly, the stomach juice and stomach activity are important.

Does it matter if the pancreas does the digestion rather than the mouth and stomach? What difference does it make if protein is digested by the alkaline pancreatic juices or the stomach acid?

There are two important differences. There is slower digestion because the food gets bogged down in the stomach, and there is less complete digestion. These two factors are the root causes of the smothering of the healing process, and thus the beginning of disease. When the digestion is quickened and made more complete, the body immediately reactivates its healing powers.

PATIENTS' LETTERS

My daughter Heather, age 11, first had unexplained illnesses when she was 9. The stomach aches and migraine headaches kept her home from school often in October of 1985. Then she got the chicken pox in November. That went away, but she still had the stomach aches and migraines, and then also neck and shoulder pain. In January, she began to have ringing and pain in her ear, as well as hearing loss. Up to this point the doctors had her in for X-rays, Ultra Sound and blood tests, and she was on Tylenol Extra Strength, Tylenol 3, and Ergomar (to constrict cranial blood vessels). The Ear, Nose and Throat doctor ordered a Catscan, thinking she could have a cyst on the nerve to the eardrum. All tests showed that there was nothing wrong with her, but she felt worse than ever. Our G.P. started her on massage therapy for "stress". That did nothing for her. A physiotherapist said that the chicken pox virus had never left, and her treatments relieved much of the pain.

In February, Heather got strep throat, for which another antibiotic was prescribed. Four days later she could not see out of her left eye. Our doctor's office was tired of seeing us by now and very rudely told us the doctor was too busy to see Heather. She then had an allergic reaction to the antibiotic. We then insisted that our G.P. send her to an allergist. The stomach aches and migraines continued until the allergist sorted out her problems with mold, mildew, dust, and the sun. Sudden changes of temperature, such as being hot and diving into the pool, were found to trigger the migraine headaches.

Up to this point Heather had been to three G.P.'s, one allergist, two pediatricians, two Ear, Nose and Throat specialists, one physiotherapist, one massage therapist and two chiropractors. She had the above-mentioned tests and many prescription drugs. Over the sum-

mer she had to quit the swim club because of the migraines and now, breathing problems when swimming. Last fall our new family doctor took her off milk. She was better but not great. In January this year she only made it to school four days. First there was an ear infection (two antibiotics), then the flu, then tonsillitis (another antibiotic).

In February, I decided to take a different route. I had no idea what a Naturopath did, but a friend recommended Dr. Jonn Matsen. Heather started to improve about two weeks after her first visit to him. She looks so healthy now and feels fantastic. She said a few weeks ago that she had no idea that people could feel as well as she does now. She thought that everyone had aches and pains all the time but that they just didn't say anything. She thought it was normal to feel a pain in her head or her stomach and feel generally not well. She only complained when she really felt awful. We are all delighted to have Heather smiling and happy now. No more doctors, antibiotics, or endless days in bed for her. Her allergies have nearly all disappeared and she is back at swim club. She is now enjoying life without drugs and is very happy. Thank you, Dr. Matsen.

Elaine Reid
North Vancouver, B.C.

For almost three years I had no health. I was tired, helpless with extreme digestive spasm, unbearable migraine headaches, sleeplessness, and no strength. My doctor sent me to nerve specialists and others but after many tests they could find nothing wrong with me.

I was told by someone to see the Naturopath who is Dr. Matsen. I came to see him and was told to go on a certain diet and some herbs and some hydrotherapy treatments.

I started his treatments but my pain was still so severe and spread to my chest so that I was afraid that I was having a heart attack. I went back to my Medical Doctor and he sent me to a heart specialist and after tests he said there was nothing wrong with me. My doctor finally said that I shouldn't see him so often as the Medical Plan had spent over fifteen thousand dollars on specialists and diagnostic test *and they thought I was abusing the system. Yet nothing at all had been done for me. I was just as sick and miserable.*

I went back to see Dr. Matsen and after an exam he told me my new chest pain was not from my heart but from a rib that was out of place and sent me to a chiropractor, Dr. Robson, whom I also began to see.

Dr. Matsen did something to my stomach with an instrument he has and after the first hydrotherapy there was not much improvement. The second day he said "tonight you will sleep." Well, before this I had been awake continuously for months with unbearable migraines but that night I slept and have slept well since. And the headaches have gone from the diet and and the chest pain is gone from the chiropractor and I have my strength back and have lost weight and have nearly completely recovered my health so I am thanking these two doctors Dr. Matsen, the Naturopath, and Dr. Robson the Chiropractor.

May God bless their hands always as they are now.

S.P.
North Vancouver, B.C.

CHAPTER 2

The Intestines

The food moves down the duodenum into the rest of the small intestine, which is twenty feet long and lies in the middle of the abdomen in coils. The walls of the small intestine secrete further alkaline digestive enzymes which continue the breaking down of

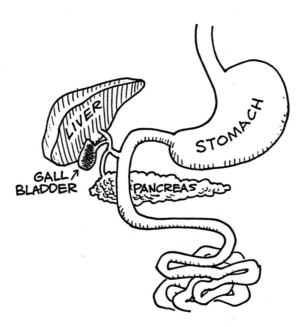

proteins into amino acids, of the long fatty chains into fatty acids, and of the starches and complex sugars into glucose.

The inner surface of the small intestine is covered with millions of tiny villi which dramatically increase the surface area of the small intestine. Like palm trees waving in the breeze, they are constantly moving, "sucking" up the small digested food particles. Each villus

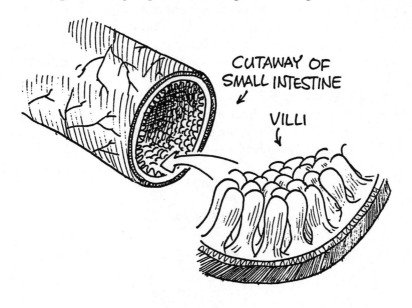

CUTAWAY OF
SMALL INTESTINE

VILLI

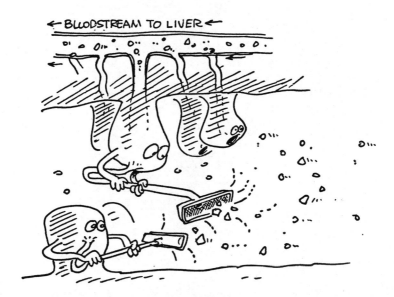

BLOODSTREAM TO LIVER

has lymph vessels which pick up fat, and veins which pick up the other digested nutrients. The veins gradually join together until they form one large vein called the portal vein, which goes directly to the liver. The fat is picked up by the lymph system instead of by the portal vein, because too much fat interferes with both liver and red blood cell function.

At the end of the small intestine is a circular valve called the ileocecal valve. This is usually kept closed so that the food stays in the small intestine long enough to be digested and absorbed fully, and also to prevent the micro-organisms in the large intestine from getting into the small intestine where their waste products could easily be absorbed. As digestion and absorption are completed the ileocecal valve opens and the smooth, rhythmic waves of contraction called peristalsis move the food into the cecum, which is the beginning of the five-foot-long large intestine or colon.

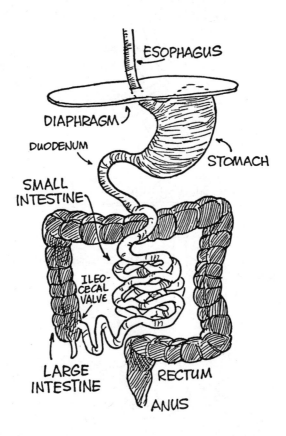

INTESTINAL FLORA

The large intestine isn't a sterile place. There are over four hundred different types of micro-organisms found there which together are called the intestinal flora. Most of them are our little friends, important aids to the digestive process. They make B-vitamins for us. They make lactic acid, which improves digestion of foods and increases absorption, as well as aiding peristalsis of the intestine. They make vitamin K, which aids in blood clotting. They make chemicals which are healing to the large intestine, and their secretions hinder the "bad guys". After they die they still help us because their bodies provide much of the bulk of a stool. There is much more to be learned about the benefits of our "little buddies".

Since it has billions of micro-organisms in residence whose waste products might inadvertently get absorbed into the portal vein, the large intestine doesn't absorb as actively as the small intestine.

When the food enters the cecum it is liquid. It gets squeezed up and down the ascending colon by peristalsis a few times, and as it moves along the transverse colon liquid is extracted. By the time it is in the descending colon, it is beginning to get the harder consistency of a stool.

"Patients with hypochlorhydria (low stomach acid) have higher bacterial counts and anaerobes(bacteriodes) and coliforms not usually found in the normal stomach." (Human Intestinal Microflora in

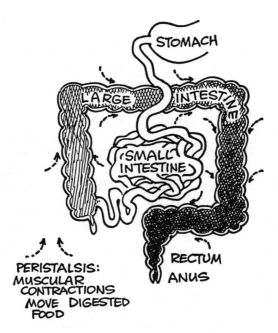

STOMACH

LARGE INTESTINE

SMALL INTESTINE

RECTUM
ANUS

PERISTALSIS:
MUSCULAR
CONTRACTIONS
MOVE DIGESTED
FOOD

Health and Disease, 1983). So we see that if the stomach doesn't work properly, there will be micro-organisms from the large intestine getting into the stomach and small intestine, rather than just in the large intestine where they belong.

While poor digestion leads to the spread of flora, other influences can lead to imbalances of the types of intestinal flora. Quoting further from the same source:

"There is convincing evidence that the indigenous intestinal flora provide natural protection against infection by a number of pathogenic bacteria. The protective mechanism is impaired, however, when antimicrobial agents are administered. Antibiotics frequently produce profound changes in the composition of the human intestinal microflora, permitting overgrowth of resistant endogenous bacteria or colonization by exogenous organisms acquired from the environment. Once resistance is reduced by antibiotic administration, even a small number of pathogenic organisms can produce serious infections in the host. Clearly, the integrity of the intestinal flora is important to the well-being of the host, and antibiotics, which upset it, should be used with extreme caution".

Chlorine is added to drinking water to kill bacteria. Does it also affect the intestinal flora? What about the thousands of other chemcals that have found their way into the food chain? Someday we will know their effect on humans, but right now we're guinea pigs. It may turn out that our long-range ability to resist these chemicals will be in direct proportion to the resistance of our intestinal bacteria.

YEASTIES AND OTHER BEASTIES

Controversy has raged within conventional medicine over Candida yeast. One school of thought says that conventional medical treatment involving medications and ignoring lifestyle has resulted in Candida yeast overgrowths in the great majority of the population. Yeast toxins can cause virtually any disease anywhere in the body. This view has been met with contempt by most of the mainstream practitioners, who ignore the volumes of evidence (see the books The Yeast Connection, Back to Health and The Yeast Syndrome) and who keep practising the same way they learned in medical school.

My clinical experience verifies that of the yeast-oriented school of thought, and perhaps the extent of the problem is even under estimated. Virtually every patient I've had has benefited to some degree from using yeast killers. This would indicate clearly to me that every one of us has an overgrowth of yeast, whether or not it is active enough to cause symptoms or to show on conventional tests.

While drugs and refined modern foods are now blamed as the major causes of the yeast problem, I find that that isn't so. Drugs and refined foods have greatly contributed to the problem, but they are of recent origin. The underlying problem goes back thousands of years. Faulty digestion is the true cause. If you don't digest your food quickly some micro-organism will digest it for you, making toxins. Antibiotics and refined foods have just recently given yeast an advantage over many of the other toxin-producing micro-organisms.

However, while yeast is presently in the limelight, it is important to remember that it isn't alone. There are hundreds of other critters with them that can make toxins, and even "good" bacteria can make toxins under certain conditions. The purpose of this book is to help you avoid these conditions. With a little understanding of how digestion works, digestion can be quickly improved and then the yeast can readily be gotten rid of permanently.

When you put slow digestion together with hungry critters you've got problems. Would you leave food lying around in a dark, damp, warm germ-infested tube for a day or more? Not if you're smart. The nasty little guys would gladly digest anything that you're slow to digest. To add insult to injury, they spew their excretions out into your intestine. They make at least seventy-eight different types of toxins. Skatols, indols, phenols, alcohol, ammonia, acetaldehyde, even formaldehyde are a few of them.

These toxins can prevent good bacteria from returning, and can provide a comfortably toxic environment that invites any other bad

guys to come on down and make themselves at home. That's another reason why we're so vulnerable when we go to the tropics. Not only do we not have the stomach juices to kill off the organisms in food, but when the organisms get into the intestine they are met with welcoming arms by our already-well-established co-hosts, the toxin-producing flora.

Many people have accumulated an assortment of intestinal critters that would make the bar scene in Star Wars look tame in comparison. Bad bacteria abound and yeast has risen high in the popularity charts. Giardia, Campylobacter, Amoebas and Yersinia are not members of the Mafia but they are members of the intestinal mob that can disrupt the peace in your intestine. Some people even pick up larger organisms such as worms, or have provided such a comfortable environment for the yeast that they can become extremely noxious fungi. You seldom find just one type of bad guy, as they provide co-operative housing for the whole nasty family. It's not that hard to get rid of them, if you get the stomach working first. If you don't, they just keep coming back again and again virtually as fast as you can kill them off.

Often associated with fermentation and putrefaction toxins are large quantities of gas. Bloating, burping, belching and flatulence are familiar signs that the little guys are blowing bubbles. For some people the formation of toxins is a quieter process, with few of the bubbly risings.

Still, as long as there are nasty hitchhikers within us, and as long as they are well-fed, the formation of toxins goes on. If the mem-

brane of the intestine gets irritated, it may secrete more mucous as
protection against the irritants. This can eventually create a thick
coat on the membrane, which will reduce the absorption of toxins.
Of course the absorption of nutrients will be reduced as well.

If the intestine gets even more irritated, inflammation will ensue.
Inflammation is one of the body's standard reactions to irritation. It
basically consists of sending more blood to the area, to flush away
the irritants and to increase the supply of nutrients and white blood
cells to speed healing. If the irritants are being produced faster than
the blood can remove them, the inflammation can become chronic.

Diseases of inflammation are usually named with the suffix-itis.
So inflammation of the colon is called colitis. If the inflammation is
in the sinuses it's called sinusitis; if it's in the bronchials it's called
bronchitis; and if it's in the joints it's called arthritis. However,
since the irritants are in the blood, the whole body is being subjected
to irritation. It is just the weaker links that are manifesting symptoms.

During inflammation, the "pores" of the intestine can become enlarged. This is called porous bowel syndrome. The enlarged pores allow the large incompletely-digested protein chunks we talked about
previously to be absorbed into the blood. This can be a major factor
in the triggering of allergies.

The standard treatments for inflammation are antibiotics if there is a bacterial infection behind them, or anti-inflammatory drugs if the irritant cause is of more mysterious origin. The strongest anti-inflammatory drug is cortisone. Cortisone often stops inflammation, but remember that inflammation is the body's natural reaction to irritation. So once you've stopped the body's natural reaction to irritation, have you stopped the irritants? Not usually. Going off the anti-inflammatories usually results in a return of the inflammation.

As we have have recently learned, antibiotics and cortisone are now believed to suppress the proper intestinal flora, so it looks like the medical profession is creating its own business by turning short-term suppression of inflammation into chronic disease. Obviously, antibiotics and anti-inflammatories belong in Emergency Medicine rather than General Practise.

Since antibiotics and anti-inflammatories are among the keystones of medicine, how can one even consider doing without them? Well, how about enabling the body's own immune system to work better, and how about stopping the cause of the inflammation?

An irritated intestine will often develop diarrhea as an attempt to flush out the irritants. Constipation is a common result of poor diet, digestion and intestine function. Treating only one of these factors usually gives only a partial improvement. Of course, the more constipated a person is, the more time for the "bad guys down-stairs" to do their nasty work, and the more time for their toxins to be absorbed into the bloodstream.

While the intestinal flora are confined to the intestine in a healthy person, "Debilitated patients . . are especially prone to infections caused by bacteria of their own indigenous flora. Immunosuppressive chemotherapy and oral antibiotic treatment synergistically promote the translocation of certain indigenous bacteria from the G.I. tract." This quote from Human Microflora in Health and Disease tells us that even the good little guys can become the bad guys if things get really tough down in the digestive tract.

I find not only that nearly everyone's stomach is underfunctioning due to chronic dietary irritation, but also that nearly everyone's intestinal flora are imbalanced, overgrown with "the bad guys".

These critters of malcontent have sometimes spread from the large intestine into the small intestine, and even into the stomach. In more severe cases they may actually get out of the intestinal tract and affect any part of the body. They throw what amounts to "a great party", and you're their host and benefactor.

Virtually everyone has an overstressed, underfunctioning digestive system, imbalanced intestinal flora, and a steady load of intestinal toxins seeping into the bloodstream. So what's the difference between someone who has actual "disease" symptoms and someone who can still eat anything without noticeable ill effects? The difference has a lot to do with the liver and gallbladder.

PATIENTS' LETTERS

I had had over a year of pain, diarrhea and blood in my stool which my G.P. (an M.D.) did not succeed in diagnosing. She re-

ferred me for a G.I. examination, and this, too, revealed nothing of value. Next, I went to a prevention oriented medical doctor who had my stool cultured for infection, and Yersinia was discovered. He told me that there were no reliably successful drugs to treat this condition.

I went to Dr. Matsen with the encouragement of my Medical Doctor. After an intensive naturopathic regime of dietary changes, naturopathic medications, self-applied acupressure and a course of hydrotherapy treatments, I was completely free of symptoms and there was no blood in my stool. My Medical Doctor was as delighted as I when, after a later follow-up stool culture, I remained free of this infection.

Sue Tauber
Vancouver, B.C.

In the spring of '84, being averse to suggested diagnosis and treatment of the allopathic method for a suspected colonic polyp, I went to see Dr. Matsen.

After one month of his dietary system my painful abdominal gas had almost disappeared. Within six months my blood pressure was normal and the "bulge" I'd battled hopelessly for fifty years was disappearing. All this and I was eating more of the foods I had been avoiding because they were considered fattening. The diet and supplements have given me two and a half great years and I look forward to many more.

Gratefully-
A. M. Fraser
Vancouver, B.C.

CHAPTER 3

The Liver, Gallbladder and Kidneys

The blood from the intestinal tract, with its rich and varied load of nutrients, toxins, chunks and possibly good/bad flora goes directly to the liver, via the funneled-down blood supply called the portal vein.

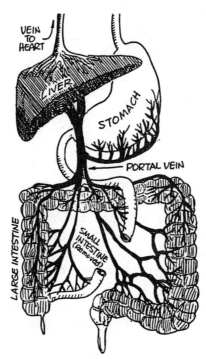

The liver is firstly a massive filter, the major filter of the blood stream. It screens everything in the blood entering it. Most toxins are immediately set upon by liver cells in order to de-activate them. The difference between a person with symptoms and one without is often related to whether the liver can handle intestinal toxins and still have enough capacity left to do its other jobs.

The liver is not only the detoxifier of poisons of intestinal origin. Heavy metals such as aluminum, copper, lead, mercury, and cadmium that find their way into the blood should be de-activated by the liver. Coffee toxins, alcohol, nicotine, drugs, pesticides, and additives should also be broken down quickly by the liver. A liver overloaded with intestinal toxins is more vulnerable to the cumulative effects of these.

In effect the liver is the main regulator of the blood. It regulates contents of blood including sugars, fats, protein and hormones,

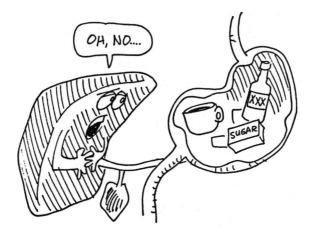

which are messengers from other parts of the body. Many of the symptoms of disease are a result of the liver being unable to regulate properly due to an overload of toxins, many of which come from fermentation or putrefaction in the intestines.

The liver regulates the blood sugar level, along with the pancreas and the adrenal glands. Glucose sugar in the blood is the common fuel for all the cells. While some parts of the body can turn proteins or fats into glucose, the brain's only fuel is from the blood glucose, so it is especially important for the brain to have the proper amount of blood glucose. If there is too little sugar in the blood, and the brain doesn't get enough nutrition, symptoms of lightheadness, anxiety, panic, weakness, dizziness, even fainting can occur. This is called hypoglycemia. Fainting is the body's way of laying the body horizontal so blood can flow into the brain without fighting against gravity, thus taking more sugar and/or oxygen to the brain.

If the sugar level gets too low, the adrenal glands secrete hormones, which stimulate the liver to release glycogen (dried glucose) from storage (add water and stir), releasing glucose into the blood. Since too much sugar in the blood can cause numerous problems (diabetes), the pancreas secretes insulin to tell the liver to remove glucose from the blood (wring the water out) and to store it as glycogen.

The regulation of the blood sugar level should be so smooth that we can go several days without eating and still not experience any major symptoms of high or low blood sugar levels. However, the brain tends to function a little better at a higher blood sugar level. We feel a little better when the glucose level is at a high level. Our

"high society" has found a number of favourite ways of forcing up the blood sugar levels.

Refined sugar, coffee, tobacco, tea, chocolate, alcohol, drugs, and emotional excitement can raise the blood-sugar levels and help us to feel good. The problem is that the pancreas and liver will immediately try to decrease the sugar to a safer level. The resultant drop in blood sugar results in a craving for more sweets, coffee, alcohol, cigarettes, drugs or emotional tirades.

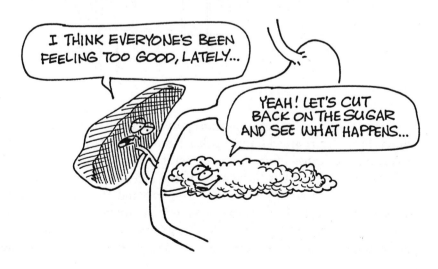

An interesting example of the relationship between these is seen at some Alcoholics Anonymous meetings, where the deleterious effects of alcohol may have been replaced with tremendous use of other stimulants such as coffee, sugar and tobacco, which may not have as bad an effect on the emotions but can be equally destructive physically.

This roller-coaster effect puts an incredible stress on the triad of pancreas, liver and adrenals, and eventually they can break down under the strain. In addition, if the liver is bogged down with an overload of intestinal toxins, its ability to regulate blood sugar can be greatly affected.

One of the liver's other important jobs is to regulate the fats in the blood. Since heart attacks and strokes from fat build-up in the arteries are a major cause of death and disability, this has received a lot of publicity. The idea that hardening of the arteries begins in old age has long been known to be wrong. In Korea and Vietnam autopsies showed that most of the teenage American troops already had fat lining the arteries to the heart, so this problem starts in childhood. Unfortunately the first symptoms may be too late a warning, as the problem usually isn't detectable until the arteries are considerably blocked.

While fats in the diet have received a lot of bad press, the major overlooked cause of fat problems is actually inadequate liver and gallbladder function. The liver and gallbladder regulate blood fat levels. When these organs are rendered sluggish by intestinal toxins, they don't regulate adequately. This is the single most important cause of high blood fat levels.

An unexpected clinical finding is that some vegetarians have actually developed chronic infections from a deficiency of cholesterol. A certain amount of cholesterol appears necessary to manufacture hormones that are essential for regulation of homeostasis.

Another of the liver's jobs is the regulation of blood-protein levels. If the protein levels are too low, the liver assembles protein "trains" from the various amino acid "cars" and dumps them into the main blood stream for distribution throughout the body. If the liver doesn't make protein properly, wasting of muscle is the most obvious sign.

The last of the main substances that the liver regulates is hormones. Hormones are messengers secreted by glands which travel through the blood to tell cells what they should be doing, to help maintain smooth functioning of all the cells together. Thus hor-

mones are important to help coordinate body homeostasis. If the hormones were allowed to keep circulating indefinitely, their messages would become out-of-date. Therefore, the hormones have to be broken down regularly. Since the liver filters all the blood in the body, it is the appropriate organ to break down most of these messengers. Poor liver function can result in sluggish hormone breakdown. Since the hormones then circulate through the blood system an extra time or two, they stimulate the cells longer than they should, disturbing homeostasis.

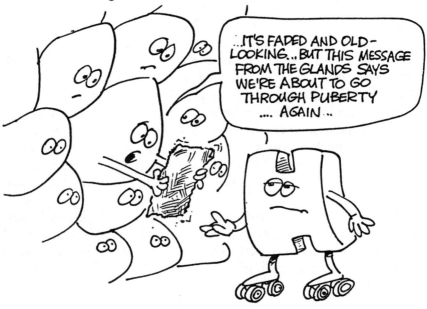

An obvious example of this is seen in men whose livers were damaged by drugs and who then developed breasts. It is also seen commonly in pubescent boys whose livers may not be damaged, but whose liver function is affected enough that the increase in hormones causes breast enlargement. The signs of hormonal imbalance are seen especially in women. The bloating, breast tenderness and mood changes of premenstrual syndrome (PMS) are symptoms that usually vanish quickly with improved liver function. Irregular menstrual cycles and menstrual cramps can sometimes be eliminated if proper liver function can be attained.

THE LIVER AS METABOLIC DIRECTOR

"Doctor, I'm so tired." That is the complaint a naturopathic physician hears most frequently. Fatigue is very common.

If we look at the liver as being a powerhouse, we will realize that we can only throw sand in it for only so long before the energy output decreases. While there are many causes of fatigue, the factor that leads to improved energy the quickest and most reliably is improved liver function. Decreasing the intestinal-toxin load on the liver usually allows it to quickly spring back to life, with a resultant increase in energy.

The metabolic rate has long been known to be regulated by the hormones from the thyroid gland, and synthetic thyroid hormone is commonly used to replace that not produced by a sluggish thyroid. Some popular books would have you believe that half the population

have a genetically weak thyroid that requires us to take synthetic thyroid hormone the rest of our lives. However, since the liver is the main regulator of the blood, it is the true key to proper metabolic rate. A sluggish thyroid is often secondary to a long-term sluggish liver. The trick to improving the thyroid permanently is to first improve the liver. To do that, improve digestion.

In the same way that the body knows what temperature it should maintain and the millions of minute steps which must be taken to keep the temperature at that point, the body also knows exactly what weight it should be and how to get there. There is no need to waste your precious brain cells and their low-voltage currents on trying to force your body into your own fashion-forged image of what you should look like. Get the liver and gallbladder working, and exercise regularly and the body will magically mold itself into shapes and forms beyond the limits of your imagination, without mental contortions and wasted effort. You may not look as anorexic as fashion temporarily would like, but your increased vitality will shine through no matter what genetic frame you have. Aim for health, and true beauty and weight control will eventually follow.

MOODINESS

In the same way that the liver regulates physical substances, it also regulates moods. The natural demeanour of a human being is positive, cheerful and stable. When the liver gets fouled up, anything can happen. Depression, pessimism, irritability, and rapid mood fluctuations are keynotes to problems of the liver. Improvement in digestion may relieve the liver of this burden, and the

brightening of personality will follow, especially in children, since they haven't had time to become accustomed to the role of the old grump as so many adults have.

In the same way that the intestinal blood flows to the liver, so does the blood in the veins. If the liver is overloaded, then the blood in the veins tends to back up, causing increased pressure on the walls of the veins. If this increased pressure is combined with weakened vein walls due to poor mineral and/or vitamin absorption, the walls may dilate. Thus liver overload can be expected when vein signs appear, such as varicose veins, hemorrhoids and dark blue bags under the eyes.

Altogether the liver has some five hundred known physical functions.

Though the liver is programmed to perform its multitude of jobs flawlessly, many people have an overloaded, malfunctioning liver. Many of my patients have a number of symptoms, but have just come from routine physical exams, blood tests, ultra sound tests and CAT scans and since nothing has been found they have been told that nothing is wrong with them. They know better, as verified by the more subtle types of energy examination. Most people with a medical symptom are found to have an overloaded liver, and/or gallbladder. Many people without symptoms do as well. The best proof of this is the sometimes dramatic improvement of symptoms as therapy improves liver function, as you will see in Part II.

LIVER TESTS

How could high-tech western medicine have overlooked such a common problem as an overloaded liver? Diagnosis in western medicine is based primarily on tissue conditions. If tissue shows no sign of damage, it's considered to not have a problem. Therefore lab work, X-rays, CAT scans, etc. have been developed to pick up these damaged states. In China, however, for over three thousand years physicians cared little about tissue. Chinese physicians were aware that the energy of an organ would be imbalanced long before the organ itself would show any physical signs of malfunction. They would attempt to maintain energy balances, to prevent damage to the organs. It was considered to be a poor physician who would allow his patient to degenerate to the point that he would develop physical pathology.

The standard screening test for liver problems in western medicine is a blood test that looks for liver enzymes in the blood. Since the enzymes are normally contained within the liver cells, this test will only spot liver trouble after the liver cells have been ruptured, spilling their enzymes into the bloodstream. This is a wonderful test to pick up liver damage, but worthless to pick up early-stage liver overload. Unfortunately for the patient with early-stage functional problems, most doctors ignore their complaints if nothing shows on the standard lab tests.

PATIENTS' LETTERS

I have suffered with high blood pressure for more years than I can remember. I have spent a small fortune on drugs or so-called medications which never seemed to do any good. What I went through would take too long to repeat, so I will just start in January of 1987 when I had another of many severe dizzy spells I have had over the years. As usual I was bed-ridden for two weeks. If I tried to stand I fell and felt as though I was spinning around. After two weeks the dizziness stopped so I started trying to move around and get my strength back. It took me two months before I could take a short walk. My blood pressure was getting higher and higher, so I finally decided enough is enough, no more drugs that did nothing but give me a lot of side effects. I quite honestly thought that this time I was not going to get better.

In desperation or maybe fate, I looked in the "Yellow Pages" under Naturopaths and saw Dr. Matsen's name. I phoned and made an appointment. It was the best thing I have ever done.

I had a blood test, muscle testing, food sensitivity testing and a long talk with the doctor, who explained everything that was happening in my body in a simple way that I could understand. He told me which foods I shouldn't eat, and gave me some botanical remedies and a course of hydrotherapy.

After three days I began to feel better. After one month I felt like a different person. The chronic headaches I had had for years disappeared, along with blurred vision, pains in my legs, back and neck, etc.

My own M.D. couldn't believe it and was horrified at what I was doing, but after the first month of rapidly-decreased blood pressure he wished me well.

I will never be able to thank Dr. Matsen enough for what he has done for me.

I think each and every one of us should be able to choose which type of doctor is best for us and be covered for all treatments by medical insurance.

Alma Crighton
North Vancouver, B.C.

Before I came to see Dr. Jonn Matsen, I had trouble with my legs, especially my left side. Intermittently, they became stiff and weak. I gradually could not walk very far. At one stage, it was so bad that I could hardly make a 100-yard distance. My orthodox doctor could not pinpoint the cause of my complaint, but suspected that I had hardening of the arteries. This diagnosis could not be established until I was willing to go through an angiogram test. To avoid the ordeal of such a process, I decided to consult a naturopathic doctor.

I was strongly recommended by some of my friends to see Dr. Matsen. So I made an appointment on 20 May, 1986 to be at his clinic. On examining me, Dr. Matsen found that I had too much *toxin in my blood and fat from a sluggish liver. I went through a food sensitivity test which revealed sensitivities to certain foods like peanuts, tea, yeast and mushrooms.*

Based on the results of all these tests, he started to treat me stage by stage. First of all, a list of proper food combinations was given to me. I was advised to follow according to the instructions printed therein. At the same time, I underwent a hydrotherapy period. My blood was tested several times as my treament progressed. Dr. Matsen then gave me a course of caprylic acid to be taken for 16 days. This was to get rid of the yeast in my system. On my 11th visit during the first week of July, I was happy to know from the blood test that my system was cleansed of the toxin by 75%.

Ever since I was under Dr. Matsen's care, I have found that my health has improved tremendously. I can walk the normal distance as I used to do before, in fact much better than I expected. Here is an instance that has shown a marked improvement in me. Recently, I resumed my golf game. To my utter astonishment, I could complete a round of 18-hole golf without feeling tired. My legs gave me no trouble at all. Normally, I felt rather exhausted by the time I approached the 8th hole and I had to stop playing after a 9-hole round.

Another very heartening discovery is that my angina pains have more or less disappeared. I used to suffer from chest pains after a meal and also when I climbed long flights of steps. Now it looks that such complaints are something of the past.

With the new life-style which I have adopted through Dr. Matsen's guidance, I am now enjoying a newfound vibrant energy.

Diana Ng
North Vancouver, B.C.

―――――――

THE GALLBLADDER

The liver filters and neutralizes the toxins, before concentrating them into bile. If bile is needed immediately in the small intestine to help emulsify fat, it is secreted from the liver through the bile ducts into the duodenum, just below the stomach. Bile also helps lubricate the intestine and gives the stool a golden color. Lack of bile gives the stool a light or clay color. If surplus bile is made it is shunted into the gallbladder, where storage turns it a darker color.

The conventional surgical viewpoint is that the gallbladder is as disposable as the tonsils and appendix were once thought to be. That is simply not so. My observations, based on clinical experience, tell me that good quality bile from the liver and gallbladder is of extreme importance to health.

However, to show that research is finally catching up with common sense I include the following quote:

"The yellow pigment in bile that causes the characteristic yellowing of jaundice sufferers may not be simply a body waste after all, scientists say. Bilirubin, long thought to have no value, may be beneficial in thwarting cancer, aging, inflammation and other health problems, researchers from the Berkeley and San Francisco campuses of the University of California have found. The researchers say bilirubin appears to be a powerful antagonist of oxygen compounds that play a role in numerous diseases and conditions. Roland Stocker, the lead investigator in the study, said the results indicate scientists should examine other wastes from chemical processes in the body to see if they also have other functions. Reporting in the most recent issue of Science, Stocker and his associates said in test-tube studies, bilirubin acted much like ant-oxidants vitamin C and E, neutralizing so-called oxygen radical compounds that destroy beneficial vitamin A and linoleic acid, a common fatty acid that is a major component of cell membranes. 'Instead of spending 95% of our time developing means to get rid of bilirubin, we should spend time on possible beneficial roles of bilirubin,' Stocker said." (Vancouver Sun, March 7, 1987). "Human Intestinal Flora in Health and Disease," speculates, "Secondary bile acids may very well be responsible for protection against a variety of enteric (intestinal) infections."

The two most important things to remember from this article are the effects of bilirubin on free radical oxygen compounds and on fatty acids. For decades western medicine has overlooked the obvious connection between lifestyle and disease, in the same way that primitive tribes couldn't see the connection between sex and babies. They seemed too remote and separated to be connected. However, the two most important missing links between diet and disease have been found recently. They are free radicals and prostaglandins.

Gallbladder problems start when the liver is so overloaded with intestinal toxins that they get dumped into the duodenum or gallbladder before they are fully neutralized. These toxins, if left simmering in the gallbladder, can cause so much irritation that the gallbladder begins to malfunction. If the gallbladder doesn't secrete bile properly, the fats and minerals in the bile can become stones. The most common symptom associated with gallbladder trouble is feeling worse after eating fatty foods.

If toxic bile is secreted from either the liver or gallbladder into the intestine, it can cause aggravation throughout the gastro-intestinal tract. The already "shocked" stomach can get even more aggravated. Many people who think they have stomach problems or duodenal ulcers may actually get these symptoms from toxic bile, which creates "hot" spots.

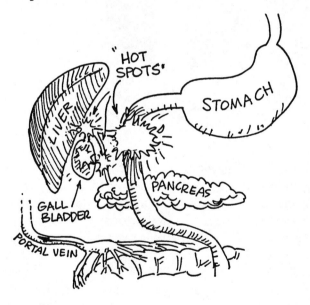

The majority of heart problems are caused by gallbladder trouble. Low-cholesterol diets have missed the boat as the body can make cholesterol even faster than it can extract it from food. When the liver and gallbladder are improved they can control the blood fat levels as they were designed to do. The best way to regain liver and gallbladder function is to stop overloading them with toxins.

Reference to an acupuncture clock shows that it is the gallbladder meridan that controls the heart meridan. It also plays an important role in immunity, by its impact on fat absorption and resultant effect on membrane strength, which is important for cell defense.

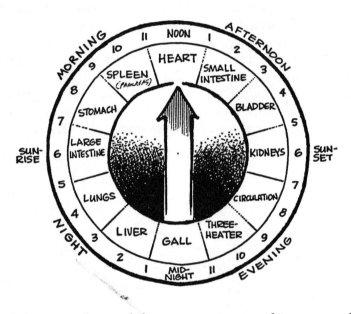

When you understand the acupuncture meridians you realize that the toxic gallbladder is often the cause of migraines, chronic neck problems, some knee problems and most skin problems.

The liver can be overloaded whether or not there are symptoms. Once the liver's capacity to detoxify is overwhelmed, toxins can spill past the liver into the main bloodstream. There are even some intestinal toxins that the liver is incapable of filtering, which get into the main bloodstream regardless of the function of the liver.

Once the toxins are in the main bloodstream the kidneys are the only filters left that can de-activate them. The kidneys, however, aren't well-suited to this task. Irritation throughout the kidneys, bladder and urethra may occur. This irritation can make the urinary tract more prone to infection. Also, interference with the kidney's normal functions such as regulation of fluids and minerals may occur, resulting in fluid retention and/or mineral deficiencies, or crystalization of minerals into stones.

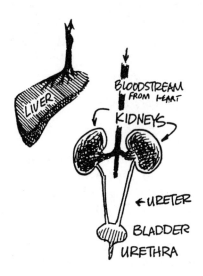

PATIENTS' LETTERS

My difficulties started in 1970. They began with inability to hold urine, which resulted in excruciating restlessness and anxiety. This caused such insomnia that I became a dopey wreck.

Urine tests showed nothing. I went back to England. Seven times they stretched my bladder. I was admitted to the emergency room for catheterization. They took kidney X-rays and repeatedly gave me antibiotics for bladder infections. I became a nervous, irrational wreck. The best doctors in Toronto, Crewe and Chester, could do nothing except recommend I take a two-year vacation. I was put on Valium, to no avail.

I remember lying in my bed looking out my window thinking that I have been ill for fifteen years. I coped, I existed but I couldn't carry on like this for another fifteen years.

When I visited Dr. Matsen, he checked me over and gave me a diet sheet indicating things I was to avoid. He also gave me some supplements which really stirred my system up. I felt rotten but not pathetic and indeed didn't get out of bed for five days. When I returned to him he gave me a homeopathic medicine which helped right away. After six months on his diet and some herbs and supplements, I sleep like a log and wake up a new person every morning.

My bladder is only a problem if I go too far off my diet. I have lost thirty-five pounds and I look good and feel wonderful.

Tell me, what are all the people in this world today who suffer the way I did, going to do without a Dr. Matsen of their own?

> Hilary C. Venecek
> North Vancouver, B.C.

I want to write and thank you so very much for all you have done to help me find the way back to good health.

In May I suddenly started retaining fluids and within two weeks I put on thirty-six pounds. My M.D. who put me on several water pills, which did not help the fluid build-up. I was finally diagnosed as having nephrotic syndrome and was hospitalized. After a kidney biopsy, a specialist told me I had focal segmental glomerulosclerosis and that nothing could be done but that he would monitor the protein loss in the urine and check for further deterioration.

Another person you helped recommended that I see you. After your testing, diet, supplements and hydrotherapy treatments I very soon began to feel better. The protein loss went from very high to minimal within three weeks. I was no longer retaining fluids.

I am now even slightly below my normal weight and I feel just great, full of energy again and living a very normal life.

> Christian J. Resch
> Surrey, B.C.

CHAPTER 4

Blood and Lymph

Once past the kidneys, there is little to prevent the toxins from circulating through the entire bloodstream, irritating the membranes of every single cell in the body. These toxins act upon the whole body, but manifest as disease wherever a person has his or her weakest link. The weakness may be caused by genetic make-up, accident or injury, nutritional deficiencies, physical or emotional stress, or psychological troubles. A person with a minor genetic weakness may develop noticeable symptons only after years of toxins aggravating that weak area.

A person with mineral deficiencies may get degeneration of the intervertebral discs, as the discs are softer and therefore more prone to erosion when deficient in manganese, cobalt, calcium and other minerals. The discs under the most physical wear and tear will likely be affected first. If there was a whiplash, that area might be the most susceptible to degeneration.

A person who is vulnerable to skin trouble due to poor fat absorption may develop eczema, as the toxins "eat their way" through the weakened skin from the bloodstream. Exposure to detergents may be blamed as the cause, but this is simply something that further weakens the skin so that the toxins "leak out". The main problem is with the blood, not with the external agent.

Another person, after years of heavy physical labour, may develope osteoarthritis as the toxins make the wear-worn joints more vulnerable to erosion.

A person with a stressed nervous system may develop a nervous disease.

A person with high blood fat and hormonal imbalance due to sluggish liver and gallbladder may develop acne.

Membranes secrete extra mucous to protect themselves from the constant irritation. If this mucous isn't drained off quickly, it can cause congestion and further aggravate poor circulation in the effected area.

Any area with decreased circulation of blood and the nutrients it should be carrying is prone to developing problems, especially if the waste removal from the area is also sluggish.

Chronic irritation makes an area hypersensitive, causing it to

react against things that normally shouldn't bother it, such as pollen, dust, feathers, furs, and certain foods. The hypersensitive area may be the nose, the lungs, or the sinuses.

In any sensitive-membrane disease, the membrane of the large intestine was irritated long before the problem manifested elsewhere. It is difficult or impossible to truly heal such problems without first correcting the intestinal problems. If digestion is improved, detoxification leads to desensitization.

Since the stomach itself is aggravated by these toxins in the blood, it too can become hypersensitive. We found earlier that the stomach is in "shock" from dietary abuse beginning in early childhood.

We also found that the stomach can be aggravated by toxic bile. Now, as the stomach becomes even more sensitive, it can react to a large number of things. Even foods that would never be suspected of being harmful to a person can aggravate the already weak digestion. The result is slower digestion, increased growth of the intestinal bad guys, more fermentation and putrefaction toxins, more liver overload and increased sensitivity. The problem becomes a vicious cycle, which can get even worse.

In my practise I use a simple blood test called the HLB test. A few drops of blood are taken on a slide so that they are one cell-layer thick. As the blood dries, the fibrin forms a net-like pattern. If there are substantial quantities of free radicals in the blood, they will tear holes in the fibrin net as the blood dries. Under microscopic magnification (200 magnification) these holes can be readily observed. Since these free-radicals are in the main blood stream, they subject every cell in the body to the same irritation that the fibrin net is receiving. This test can thus be used as a general indicator of systemic free-radical activity, though it cannot be used to diagnose any particular disease or a problem that is localized to one area and therefore not affecting the entire blood stream.

An interesting new technological addition to this test was demonstrated recently. Instead of the 200 magnification, new equipment boosted the magnification up to 6800 power. What is seen then in the blood is that the little critters that we once thought were only in the intestine are also in the bloodstream. Small "buds" of yeast are seen in almost everyone. Many people also have L-form bacteria, fungi and mycoforms. One lady, apparently in good health, actually had worms in her blood. The white blood-cell activity can also be seen and of course the more active this is, the less numerous the critters.

We truly are living in a sea of micro-organisms. A balance is in play between our immune system and these organisms, and a person with an active immune system has little to fear from these little guys. Infection is a word that must be used cautiously because many of these organisms are already found within us. An overgrowth is more of an indication of our own weakened state than a sign that these small creatures have any great powers of destruction. Many of these guys are nature's recyclers. When we are done with our bodies they convert us to plant food so that the cycle of life can continue. Unfortunately, by weakening our vitality with poor diet and faulty digestion and absorption of toxins, we weaken our immune system so the critters think we're finished with our bodies and begin the composting process before we think we're done.

Improved diet, digestion and absorption usually result in quick improvement in the blood pictures. As free-radical levels decrease, consequent improvement in disease signs and symptoms usually soon follows.

THE LYMPH SYSTEM

Much of the toxicity gets drained away through the lymphatic system. Waste drainage is so important to cell health that the lymph system is three or four times larger than the blood system. Unfortunately, it is designed to handle only cell wastes. When the blood is also dumping toxins from the intestinal tract into the lymph system via the overloaded liver, the lymph system can get overloaded too.

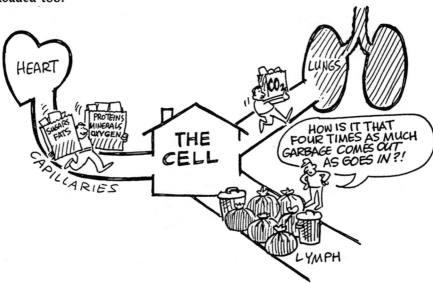

Unlike the blood system, which has the heart as a consistent built-in pump, the lymph system (like the veins) relies on the less consistently used skeletal muscle contractions to "squeeze" the lymph along.

Lack of exercise can greatly aggravate lymph overload. This sluggish lymph drainage is most commonly felt in the throat area because the lymph is closest to the surface there, but it is actually most overwhelmed in the large intestine area. Of course this is because the large intestine is where the critters are having the main party, and their "spilled drinks" are overwhelming the drain.

The lymph system is also the home turf of the immune system. Tonsils, adenoids and lymph nodes are fortresses in the lymph where the immune system attacks any invaders.

LYMPH SYSTEM

Large chunks of poorly-digested protein can be mistaken by the immune system invaders. This false alarm can result in an overly-reactive immune system which may cause allergic reactions. Overloading these lymph glands results in swelling. Enlargement of the lymph glands in the throat can block the drainage from the middle ear via the eustachian tube, since this tube enters the throat near the tonsils. The resulting congestion of the ear can lead to decreased hearing, ruptured ear membranes or ear infections.

Most people are afraid of infections, whether viral, bacterial, yeast or fungal. If the truth is known, very few of these organisms could be called contagious. Even in an epidemic it's usually only a small portion of the population that gets the disease, and an even smaller portion that succumbs to it. Most of the victims also suffer from obvious sanitation or nutritional problems, or weakened immunity due to old age, drug use, severe emotional stress or severe disease already existing. Many of the germs that people fear most have such delicate life cycles that it is only with the greatest difficulty that they can even be grown.

MEET YOUR DEFENDERS: THE WHITE BLOOD CELLS

There are monsters found in the body far more hideous and destructive than any known virus or bacteria. They lumber through the blood-stream engulfing and eating anything they don't like. They shoot bullets containing powerful toxins that can rip apart the membranes of anything that dares get in their way. They send powerful signals that invite their cronies to come scurrying to join the feast. They multiply in a day from a few to tens of thousands. They actually change shape to slip through gaps between cells so that they can attack from all sides. They have little mercy for their enemies.

Fortunately, they're on your side. They are the White Blood Cells, your defenders. They have such an amazing bag of tricks, and such overwhelming tenacity that no germ can withstand a pitched battle with these phagocytes, B-cells and T-cells, when they are in prime fighting condition.

There are trillions of these little heroes, the White Blood Cells, in your body. They have the ability to recognize what is you and what isn't and they attack with incredible ferocity.

The first on the scene is usually the macrophage, which resembles a bouncer at a late-night club: big and tough and afraid of nothing. Bacteria are eliminated as easily as you would step on an ant. Macrophages easily gulp down micro-organisms unfortunate enough to fall within their long grasp and are digested by strong enzymes. Macrophages "scalp" their victims and display this "germ skin" like a medal. This excites the Helper T-cells who run around excitedly like Olive Oyle: "Help, somebody help me".

This stimulates the B-cells and Killer T-cells to multiply and come to the assistance. With these other cells, macrophages can readily destroy many types of cancer cells.

The most numerous of your defenders are the Neutrophils. These are smaller, more nimble versions of the macrophages that specialize in tracking down and devouring bacteria.

The excited cries of the Helpers stimulate the B-cells to unleash thousands of chemical compounds per second called antibodies that work like packs of angry Pit Bulls. Though small, they're fierce; they bite hard and hang on for dear life.

This weakens the invader and also further marks it as an enemy. The antibodies pick up a series of chemicals from the blood, that can detonate, blowing a large hole in the membrane of the would-be invader.

Enter the Killer T-cells. A hush falls as they enter the duel. At first the intruders laugh because "Killer" cells look like harmless cotton balls, but behind that soft exterior is a hair-trigger hired gun.

Quick on the draw. Shoot first, ask questions never. There's a mean glint behind those eyes. Ruthless. Fortunately they're on our side. Usually. They'd be behind bars if it weren't that we needed

"REFEREE"

them at times. The bullets that the Killers fire contain chemicals that rip holes in membranes. The membranes that are attacked are yours, or at least once were, because Killer cells primarily attack cells that have been taken over by viruses or become cancer. Thus in effect the Killers are hired assassins brought in to eliminate weaklings and traitors: a dirty job, but one that has to be done. A job they do very well.

Our immune system consists of so many monsters that are so powerful and relentless that disposing of the endless array of creatures within and around us is seldom a long-term problem. Bacteria, viruses, yeast, fungi, parasites and cancer are all readily controlled by an active, alert immune system. There is even a type of cell called the Suppressor cell that goes around to simmer down an overly-exuberant immune system so that it doesn't destroy the whole body.

The body also makes Memory cells that remember particular invaders so that if they return the defenses can be activated more quickly.

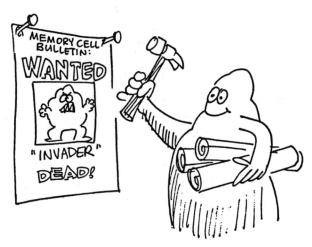

MEMORY CELL BULLETIN: WANTED "INVADER" DEAD!

THE THYMUS GLAND AND THE SPLEEN

The thymus gland and the spleen are the conductors of the "immune wars symphony".

The thymus gland is known by medicine to be responsible in early childhood for programming the T-cells to recognize foreigners, but after puberty is thought to be of little value and is still removed with little thought for consequences. A large number of children had their thymus glands treated with radiation in the fifties and sixties, and their much higher incidence of cancer shows the thymus gland's importance. The thymus gland secretes a hormone called thymosin which regulates the function of the white blood cells. The spleen is the wrecking yard of the body and should be breaking down old and damaged blood cells. Serious trouble can occur when the lymph drainage of these glands gets overloaded to the point that they malfunction and thus lose control over the T-cells. One of two things can happen.

The T-cells can become underactive. Since they protect primarily against viruses, yeast, fungi, parasites such as worms, and cancer, a person with weakened T-cell function is vulnerable to these.

The simpler types of infections, such as warts, coldsores, chronic colds and flus, yeast and fungal overgrowths such as vaginal yeast problems and athlete's foot, may be the first indications of a weakened immune system. Using energy-testing techniques, it might be estimated that about a fifth of the general population has a weakened thymus gland, often without symptoms.

In the male gay population it is probably double that number, even before exposure to the Aids virus. The higher exposure to venereal disease and the resultant increased exposure to antibiotics causes greater intestinal overgrowth, and liver and thymus overload. This in turn increases susceptibility to infections, leading to greater dependence on medications. The resulting downward spiral in health can be reversed in the earlier stages with perseverance.

A great hazard to health is when the immune system is so inactive that cancer can develop. This is the body run amok within itself, and is the most difficult of the physical problems to overcome if it affects the important organs. Underlying most cancer is long-term under-functioning of the stomach, intestinal toxicity, liver overload and a plugged lymphatic system.

However, I have seen several patients with cancer who only had a malfunctioning ileocecal valve and resultant gallbladder problems. Their weakened immunity was probably because the weakened fat absorption decreased the membrane strength of the cells so that they were less resistant in general. Unfortunately, cancer itself often generates even more toxins, which aggravate an already serious situation.

Treatment of cancer ideally should be done by those who specialize in it, whether conventionally or alternatively. Treatment of early-stage and simpler cancers by conventional treatment can often buy time to detoxify and reactivate the person's own immune system. However, most naturopaths could also give examples of patients who have had cancer reversed by activating the patient's own immune system. It takes little knowledge of how the immune system works to realize it is far easier to prevent cancer than to cure it in its advanced stages.

The other thing that can happen to the immune system is that the T-cells can become overactive. This is especially to be seen when the spleen is malfunctioning.

The white blood cells can now turn and attack the body itself. This is called auto-immune disease. It is believed there are hundreds of diseases that involve attack by the person's own defense system. Most of the diseases that have actual tissue destruction will turn out to be autoimmune disease. The ruthlessness of the Killers can be dramatic.

The classic example of autoimmunity is rheumatoid arthritis. The person's own white blood cells attack joints, resulting in inflammation. My first reversal of chronic disease by natural therapy was a case of rheumatoid arthritis. That was eleven years ago and the patient is still doing well.

While western medicine considers autoimmune diseases to be among the most serious, dramatic reversals may occur if the lymph glands can regain function, controlling the T-cells. Making changes before major damage is done, and before dependence on medication occurs, is of the utmost importance for complete reversal to be certain.

The only opponent of white blood cells that has a chance of stopping them is you. Their home base is the lymph system, but the lymph system is also the waste drainage system of the body. Obviously if the lymph system is overloaded with metabolic debris, the immune system is going to be less active. There are also specific nutrients that you have to provide for them to function properly, such as vitamins C and A and minerals such as zinc.

Studies have shown that eating white sugar and other sweets can in effect "paralyze" the white blood cells for half an hour or more. Any interference with the white blood cells' work can result in an infection or overgrowth of normal micro-organisms. The toxins produced by the infecting organism can further strain an already overloaded lymph system and make the immune system even weaker. This has been documented in "Human Intestinal Microflora in Health and Disease." (1983):

"The presence of indigenous intestinal bacteria can reduce the host immune response to certain antigens (toxins) by . . . stimulating the production of suppressor cells, indigenous intestinal bacteria can also increase the host immune responsiveness . . . by stimulating . . . Helper T-cell functions."

Antibiotics are often used at this point. They can result in remarkable improvement by killing off invading bacteria, but they have no effect on viral infections. They may also produce long-range side effects.

The good intestinal bacteria are killed off along with the bad ones when antibiotics are used. This allows yeast to multiply unchecked. The toxins that the yeast makes protect its newly-claimed territory by inhibiting the good bacteria from returning and further overloading the liver and lymphatic system. This toxic irritation causes greater hypersensitization of the body.

This vicious cycle of infection to antibiotics to hypersensitization, to more infections to more antibiotics, is especially evident in the large numbers of allergic children in North America. According to the World Health Association, sixty per cent of doctors today prescribe antibiotics for the common cold, even though they know that antibiotics do not protect against viral infections. In addition, millions of pounds of antibiotics enter our system through the food chain.

To complicate things even more, it is unlikely that a child's health would be better than its mother's.

Most young mothers breastfeed these days, but in reality they are "shooting blanks". Some of the intestinal bacteria (lactobacillus bifidus) thrive on the mother's milk and help to prepare the way for the other intestinal bacteria to be established later in life (lactobacillus acidophilus). If the mother doesn't have the proper intestinal flora (which is likely in a majority of cases) the baby is off to a poor start, and the first few rounds of antibiotics could have a deleterious effect on the child.

Evidence is also appearing that vaccinations may be causing long term immune disorders. "There are reasons for believing that immunological challenge in the form of mass vaccination programs may now be precipitating aberrant immunological effects ... in individuals who have suffered exaggerated effects from these injections of foreign disease agents". "The real danger from mass vaccines ... appears to be an indirect impairment of the immune system ... since this effect is often delayed, indirect, and masked, its true nature, is seldom recognized. (Text book of Natural Medicine. IV: Vacc Im-1-8).

PATIENTS' LETTERS

I've always been a very healthy, active person. At the age of 37 years, I began to experience periods of extreme exhaustion, anxiety, memory loss, terrible nightmares and my hair was falling out by the handful. I was unable to cope with the smallest of tasks.

After the blood tests and two very uncomfortable needles put into the thyroid gland, it was decided that I had Hashimoto's disease. For some reason my thyroid was being attacked by my own white blood cells.

I decided to find the natural way to solve this problem. Under Dr. Matsen's care a blood picture was taken which showed large amounts of fat and toxins in the blood. Food testing was done to identify foods that proved irritating to my body. I then went on a food combining diet following advice from the book Fit For Life, and had nine hydrotherapy treatments.

Within the week I began to notice improvements in energy. Weight loss came without trying.

After 5 weeks another blood picture was taken which showed great improvement. I didn't need to see this to know that I had improved because I was feeling so much better. The symptoms described above were gone.

After this I noticed a dramatic change in personality. I was so much more positive about life. I am enjoying a deep feeling of inner happiness which I haven't had for years. It's great to be alive again. All I had to do was eat properly.

Darlene Rusin
Surrey, B.C.

Lesley Colleen Worbets was born on Nov. 29, 1977, three weeks prematurely. Her birth was uneventful but she had a high level of jaundice and spent a lot of time under the "light". Blood tests continued for a week after coming home until signs of the jaundice disappeared.

Lesley was a contented baby but was very hyperactive. At 11/2 years she was very independent. In Oct. 1979 a small bald patch became noticeable on her frontal crown. This quickly spread and within fourteen days she had lost all her hair except a few wisps.

By Dec 1979 she had also lost her eyelashes and eyebrows. Numerous visits to doctors and specialists only confirmed the diagnosis of "alopecia totalis". Lesley's hair was being attacked by her own white blood cells. The prognosis was bleak-she would probably never regrow her hair. We were told to go out and buy her a wig.

Beside being bald, her hyperactivity was increasingly disruptive of the family routine. Her diet was carefully watched-sugars were eliminated as were foods containing red dye. This helped a bit.

In May 1980, a friend who was a layman natural healer saw Lesley and asked if she could help. Having nothing to lose, we said yes. Lesley was given "Bioplasma" in combination with Silicea 6x. Overnight, Lesley settled down and we couldn't believe whe was the same child. Her diet was still restricted but now we could handle her and reason with her. From this point on, things got better.

In Jan 1981, Dr. Mesery, a Naturopathic Physician, agreed to treat Lesley. His remedies included phosphorus, silicea and arsenicum in homeopathic doses. These further helped to control the hyperactivity and then the hair started growing. The patches that became bald first were the last to fill in. Lesley was very proud to see her hair growing and of course, we were delighted! The hair was very dark and wiry initially, but then it began to soften and lighten.

By Nov 1981 Lesley had a bald spot the size of a quarter on the back of her head. It was covered by other hair so was not noticeable and the frontal crown was just starting to fill in.

In June of 1982, Lesley again lost a large patch of hair at the back of her head, but by Oct. it had filled in again. During all this time Lesley continued taking Bioplasma and Silicea 6x as well as being on a sugar restricted diet.

In late 1984 Lesley again had a bald patch appear. As Dr. Mesery had retired I took Lesley to see Dr. Matsen. Besides sugar she tested sensitive to milk and yeast and most grains. These were removed from the diet and a few supplements added. Lesley's hair was soon healthy and silky.

Then on April 1, 1986 Lesley was struck down by a motor vehicle when she ran out into the street. Her injuries were not serious but she did require surgery to close a head laceration. As a result of the accident, her body was subjected to intravenous general anesthetic and antibiotics. The hospital was going to give her a tetanus shot but I refused and explained about the alopecia. They gave her a minute amount and she got an instant reaction to it (a rash on her arm at the sight of the injection) so no more tetanus was given.

About two to three weeks later a bald spot was noticed on the back of her head and within another week, noticeable thinning of the hair as well as loss of hair at the base of the skull. Dr. Matsen put Lesley on caprylic acid which arrested the hair loss and it has now regrown silky as before.

In the last seven years, the medical profession has had no explanations nor solutions to Lesley's problem. Fortunately, we discovered homeopathy and Naturopathic Medicine, and are strong believers in it.

Iris Worbets
North Vancouver, B.C.

PROSTAGLANDINS, FREE RADICALS AND ELECTRICAL ACTIVITY

What is it about a few little toxins generated by poor diet and faulty digestion that can bring about malfunction of an organism that is programmed to run flawlessly? Why should such a powerful self-regulating creature, armed to the teeth with "monsters", fall victim to indigestion? Let's take a closer look at the effects of the toxins themselves.

For hundreds of years, when people got sick they believed that they had poisons in their blood. Modern lab work couldn't find enough toxicity to cause major disease. The discovery of germs led to the ridicule of this toxicity theory. However, recent discoveries in biochemistry have found two missing links that show how small amounts of toxins can cause major problems.

One is the discovery of prostaglandins. Prostaglandins only last a fraction of a second, which is why they have only been discovered recently. In their short lives, however, prostaglandins can have a powerful effect on the body. In fact, they're believed to be the strongest compounds made by the body. In the short time that prostaglandins have been known, an incredible amount of research has been done on them. They have been implicated in dozens of diseases already, and we may expect that number to rise radically. Prostaglandin disorders have been found especially in diseases that involve circulation and immunity. Let's take a closer look at the formation of prostaglandins.

A cell membrane is composed of fats. When a hormone from a gland hits the membrane, it triggers an enzyme to turn some of the membrane fat into a prostaglandin. The prostaglandin in turn stimulates or inhibits the activity of the cell. In other words, it's an off/on switch.

Many different types of prostaglandins can be made, and a slight difference in their structure can dramatically alter their effect on the body in general. The thing that affects the type of prostaglandin the most is the type of fat found in the membrane. That depends on the type of fat in the diet and the climate that the fat was grown in. In general, the colder the climate the more unsaturated the fat. The structure of the prostaglandin changes accordingly. Since climate affects fat types, and fat types affect circulation through prosta-

glindins, obviously the idea of eating according to your climate is important.

Like everything else in life, there is good and bad in prostaglandins. While the "good" prostaglandins can have powerful beneficial impact in regulating the body in homeostasis, "bad" prostaglandins can have an equally powerful but deleterious effect on cell regulation and function. A lot of research has been done on why the harmful ones are formed. Obviously the proper fats have to be found in the membrane. These are called the essential fatty acids. These fats must be in the diet, as the body can't make them. They are found especially in flax and seafood, so these have begun to take a larger role in our diet. However one thing that is often overlooked in esssential fatty acid research is that it is important to have proper bile (liver and gallbladder function) to absorb the fatty acids.

Faulty function of the enzyme that turns the essential fatty acids into prostaglandins, delta-6-desaturase, has been blamed by some researchers as the culprit in diseases involving "bad" prostaglandins. Aspirin blocks the function of this enzyme, stopping the formation of the bad prostaglandins, which gives relief of circulation-induced pain. However, the problem is that aspirin stops the formation of the good prostaglandins as well. Since the good prostaglandins especially influence circulation and immunity, these are the side-effects that you would expect to see with aspirin use. Stomach bleeding and immune deficiencies are well-known problems with aspirin.

Alcohol is known to stimulate the enzyme delta-6-desaturase. Thus the old concept of using hot rum to burn up a cold could be true. The alcohol stimulates the enzyme to produce more prostaglandins, to increase immune function, thus destroying the cold virus overnight.

The problem is that the alcohol has a reverse effect the next day. This may be due to acetaldehyde, the chemical residue from the breakdown of alcohol that can cause hangovers. Acetaldehyde inhibits the enzyme, weakening the immune system further. If the virus wasn't killed overnight, it could come back with a vengeance.

Evening primrose oil and black currant oil were recently found to contain an oil that can become prostaglandins without needing the enzyme. Often good results can be obtained in many diseases.

However, what gives the quickest and deepest results is detoxification. This would indicate that the main interference with proper prostaglandin formation is from toxins. Of the seventy-eight known toxins that originate in the intestine, many are closely related to alcohol (phenols, indol, skatol, etc.), and since one is acetaldehyde itself, it appears that the detrimental effects of the toxins occur by their disruption of the enzyme that turns fats into prostaglandins. Since prostaglandins are so important for smooth physical function it can be seen that disruption of prostaglandin formation amplifies the effect. That is, a few toxins in the blood can result in dramatic problems in the body.

We can expect that further research will verify that this is one of the missing links in understanding how poor diet and digestion can

result in any disease anywhere in the body. Even more important, by reversing this process health may be restored.

FREE RADICALS

Another recent discovery of biochemistry is that of free radicals. Like prostaglandins, free radicals last for only a fleeting moment, but in their short life they can also have a dramatic effect on the body, though in a different fashion.

Let's consider where free radicals come from. The most important nutrient in the body is oxygen. We can live weeks without food, days without water, but only minutes without oxygen. Oxygen comes in many forms. We most commonly identify oxygen as O_2 which is the form it is usually found in in the atmosphere. In this form the two oxygen atoms are bound together by a pair of electrons that they share. O_2 is happy and content. As in a good marriage, both members are fulfilled.

If you split the two oxygens atoms apart, they end up imbalanced. One oxygen atom would have the two electrons and the other would have none.

These are called ions. The one without electrons is positively charged and the one with electrons is negatively charged. Ions are mildly reactive. That is, they are searching for fulfillment. The positive ions are searching for electrons, while the negative ions need to give them away. As they rush around searching for each other, the cell membranes "tease" them by allowing them to rush towards each other, but prevent actual fulfillment. It's this thwarted urge to become more stable that gives action to the body. Ah, the singles bar of life.

Another way to separate O_2 is to break apart the two oxygen atoms in such a way that each one gets one of the electrons. These are called free radicals. 'Radical' is the appropriate word. These molecules are so unstable that they, like prostaglandins, last only a fraction of a second. During their short life they will get an electron from somewhere, anywhere. Since normally there are few free elec-

trons in the body, they usually get them by ripping them out of membranes. Since an area of the body the size of a pinhead can have millions of these free-radical reactions per second, this can have a severely destructive effect on the cell membranes.

Fortunately, the body does have buffers against these reactions. Alpha-tocopherol (vitamin E) works like a Pacman, gobbling up free radicals. Beta-carotene, vitamin C and selenium are a few of the other nutrients in the body that help buffer free radicals.

Now we know that bile has even stronger free scavengers, which gives even more insight into the importance of proper liver and gall-bladder function. Since the white blood cells unleash free radicals on invaders to help rip apart their defensive membranes, free radicals aren't all bad. However, it's extremely important that the body keep control over free radicals. If the body loses control of the white blood cells by malfunction of the thymus gland, the extra free radicals can be too much for the buffers to handle, and irritation and eventual damage can result.

The type of membrane damaged by the free radicals determines the seriousness of the damage. The membranes surrounding the more vital internal organs are much more important than surface skin. The most serious long-range damage occurs when the genetic material within the reproductive organs is damaged, as that may be passed on for generations.

It has long been known that damage from exposure to radiation, whether from ultraviolet sun rays or from gamma rays of nuclear fission, occurs from the production of free radicals, which in turn causes the actual physical damage. Sunlight has thus been blamed as the major cause of skin cancer, but we know that moderate exposure to sunlight is healthy. The problems occur when the body is already full of internally-generated free radicals.

Where do these free radicals come from? Any of the toxins from the intestine can probably produce an abundance of them. Whether skatols, phenols, indols, ammonia, acetaldehyde, hydrogen sulphide, neurine, aminoethyl mercaptan, putrescine, cadaverine, histamine, tyramine, formaldehyde or the myriads of others, the common denominator among these physical toxins is their ability to generate large numbers of free radicals. When the buffering system is overloaded, disease occurs.

Many people force-feed the system with anti-oxidant supplements to help buffer these free radicals, and that may give good results.

The dramatic results occur, however, when the production of toxins is stopped at the source, the digestive system.

We have now finished our journey down the digestive system and learned how poor diet and faulty digestion can result in incomplete absorption of nutrients and a build-up of toxins in the blood, which can overload the liver and circulate thoughout the body causing irritation. If the immune system gets overloaded, more serious problems can result.

ELECTRICAL ACTIVITY

Let's go back to the beginning and take another look at this system, but from a different viewpoint. Instead of looking at the physical level, let's look at energy instead.

Remember the mouth makes alkaline juice, the stomach makes acid, the pancreas alkaline and the intestinal flora make acid again. This alteration of acid and alkaline may remind us of batteries. Indeed it is this battery-type system that the body uses, not to make energy but simply to extract energy from food, and to put it into acceptable form for the body to use and store.

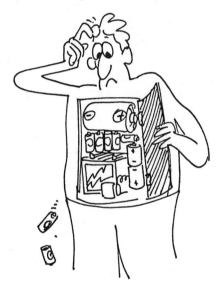

Swedish cancer researcher Dr. Bjorn Nordenstrom has recently discovered that the arteries not only carry cells and nutrients, but also a flow of electrical activity that is critical to both health and healing. He states that it is the alternating flow and ebb of positive and negative ions that carries on the natural healing process in the body. While this concept has been met with extreme skepticism by conventional medicine, alternative physicians would respond with a simple shrug that in effect says, "What took so long?"

Three thousand years ago the Chinese discovered that organs generate biomagnetic energy currents that circulate throughout the body in channels called meridians that distribute the energy to the physical body. They found that the energy is imbalanced long before the organ has problems, so they focused their treatments on maintaining energy balance. One of their insights was that the stomach meridian is one of the most important.

So the digestive system is designed to extract energy, and depends on alternation of alkaline and acid to draw the energy from the crude food mass. The greater the ability of the body to make these opposites, the greater the ability to extract energy. Perhaps we can call this the source of vitality.

The problems in this "digestive battery" occur when the digestive organs function improperly, so that instead of producing a flow of ions in the blood, the electric process "shorts out" so that free radicals circulate through the blood instead of ions. So the blood, which is supposed to nurture the cells with a bath of nutrients, is flooding the cells with a sea of irritants.

The more common digestive deficiencies are of stomach acids and intestinal acids that are supposed to be made by the intestinal flora. The result in disease is an overly alkaline or acidic state. Much has been made of acid and alkaline diets, but they are of less importance if the digestive organs are functioning properly, as the body can then regulate acid and alkaline balances better. In fact, dietary changes will usually result in little long-range improvement in health unless the digestive organs are also improved.

If the liver gets overwhelmed with free radicals and they get passed into the bloodstream, these "sparks" can ignite "spot fires" anywhere in the body if they aren't quickly squelched.

That is the beginning of disease. Disease begins with faulty digestion long before the first aches and pains, long before there are any symptoms.

The real strength of naturopathic medicine is that it includes not only diagnosing and treating conventional physical symptoms, but also interpreting and treating the earlier-stage energy imbalances. A number of energy-testing techniques such as acupuncture pulses, electro-acupuncture devices and applied kinesiology (muscle testing) have been developed to pick up these energy imbalances. Since conventional diagnosis is based on tissue pathology, these more subtle techniques do not diagnose disease as defined by these physical standards. They can be invaluable, however, in finding the true root of a patient's problems.

One hundred and fifty years ago it was discovered that each area of the body has a representative area in the iris of the eye. In effect, the iris works like a colour television screen, the cameras being

found in every cell of the body. By looking in the iris, some of the early preconditions of disease can be seen.

Since we already know that the stomach is the sparkplug of the digestive system and the hub of your body, it should come as no surprise that it is also at the center of the iris, occupying the area just outside the pupil. The intestinal area is represented just outside the stomach. Outside the stomach and intestinal area is a ring which separates these two areas from the rest of the iris, which contains the representative areas for the rest of the body.

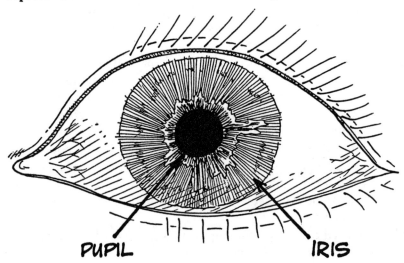

PUPIL   IRIS

If the two internal organs, the stomach and the intestine, are treated with care, it is extremely difficult for the rest of the body to have disease. However, iridology shows how early we fall out of the grace of perfect health. Most Caucasian children are born with bright, deep blue eyes. They usually maintain that clarity during breastfeeding. Once they start eating, however, the eyes often change colour very quickly. Cloudy, murky whites to yellows or oranges start to appear around the intestinal ring as the digestive system begins to get overloaded. Soon the lymphatic system struggles to drain away this metabolic debris and puffy white clouds may show in its representative area towards the outside of the iris. As the elimination organs get overloaded the body may try to push toxins out through the skin which can create a dark ring around the outside edge of the iris. If antibiotics are now used the process can be greatly amplified and what were once blue eyes may now appear any shade of grey, green or hazel. Iridology shows us that the body works like a giant reservoir that has been filling slowly with toxins for years. The childhood diseases often end with puberty as there is a hormonal "boost" of mating energy that increases the vitality. As this begins to wane in the twenties, the toxin load of the body becomes more apparent again. If this reservoir capacity is filled and the person suddenly "catches" a disease, the latest event is blamed as the cause. On looking back, it will be seen that disease is usually a culmination of events, seldom a result of a single stress or disease or infectious organism.

Poor fat handling from a sluggish liver and gallbladder can result in deposits of fat in the arteries. This can be well advanced even during the teens. The consequent poor circulation may show as a haziness around the outer edge of the iris. If minerals settle in these fat deposits they may show as a white crescent around the iris, especially in the top third which represents the head area. This marking has now been recognized by conventional medicine as the "arcus senilis".

Contrary to what some books claim, iridology is not a reliable way to diagnose specific disease, but definite insights into the preconditions of disease can be seen. With improvement of the digestive system, a concurrent clearing of the iris occurs. The sparkle of the eye and glow that exudes from a healthy person is there for all to see and makeup can only struggle to imitate it.

PATIENTS' LETTERS

I am a child care worker and I receive contracts from the Ministry of Human Resources via different private societies to work with problem children and their parents. I have been doing this and other social service work for seven years.

About a year ago, I brought a nine year old, "Robert" to see Dr. Matsen. I had been working with him for about six months with some improvement in his behaviour, but after three or four weeks under Dr. Matsen's direction there was dramatic improvement. At an earlier case conference about Robert the comment was made that he would probably end up in jail. There was general agreement about this then, but there would not be now. Robert went from being an obnoxious and hyperactive child to being a popular and non-hyperactive child. One bit of trouble he did get into after starting to see Dr. Matsen occurred at a summer camp where Robert was able to return to his earlier diet. He was kicked out of camp after five days because he had become so unruly. Robert himself, has now come to understand the importance of his diet, and cooperates accordingly.

"Richard" eleven, and "William" six, are two other children whose families cooperated with Dr. Matsen in following to some reasonable extent his directions.

Richard was years behind his chronological age emotionally and academically. I had been working with him over a two year period. Within about three weeks of seeing Dr. Matsen he lost his hyperactivity. Within three months he began showing very significant academic gains, suddenly learning to read, and rising to the top of his class in problem solving. He is still behind for his age, six months after beginning to see Dr. Matsen, but one can see he is catching up now.

William I immediately brought to Dr. Matsen upon receiving the case. He had previously been on Ritlan for hyperactivity, but his father didn't like the idea and took him off. William also lost his hyperactivity within a few weeks of seeing Dr. Matsen. Now the family says they know immediately when William sneaks anything sweet. Three or four months later Williams teacher tells me he can actually begin to work on academics now, when before his behaviour would not allow this. She is very pleased with the changes. Personally I am very pleased to see the overall family situation improve along with Williams improvement. I suspect that the stress resulting from Williams earlier behaviour could have been enough to break this particular family up.

I cannot bring my clients to Dr. Matsen without parental permission, but when I get it and receive even minimal cooperation from the family, the results are tremendous. Coming from a predominantly counselling background I am surprised, but happy, to find that about fifty per cent of the work I can do with my clients is along nutritional lines.

Tim Head
Vancouver, B.C.

As long as I can remember I've had eczema, on my hands and/or forearms. The biggest offender was dish soap. While in school I was treated with a tar based medicine at night and in the daytime wore a yellow sulphur based medicine. I had to clean my hands and arms with mineral oil.

After graduating, I worked for a medical doctor. With my hands in water a lot, they broke out. He treated me with cortisone and I

kept Keri lotion always on my skin. The cortisone kept the "hot"
flare ups controlled, though my hands were always a little broken
out.

When I married and didn't have time to lavish my hands in lo-
tion, my right hand became almost unuseable, due to the cracked,
dry, bleeding eczema. I went to a Dermatologist. He put me on
stronger cortisone (said I'd kind of built an intolerance for the
other). The stronger medication left my skin damaged and appeared
to thin out my skin. When cleared up my skin actually seemed more
easily injured -thus the eczema came back stronger.

I gave up all non-essential water contact. (My husband bathed
kids, dishes). I even wore gloves to wash my hair. I tried some natu-
ral means. Some that I remember were topical vitamin E, aloe vera
and "icing" my hands to take the itch away. I started taking oil of
evening primrose. It kept my eczema at bay -while not gone it
didn't crack and bleed often. It also cost me about $50/month.

A friend suggested I see Dr. Matsen for my eczema. I made an
appointment. I discovered my eczema (and chronic constipation)
were caused by poor food combining and yeast in my system. He
put me on a properly combined diet and a yeast killer for 21 days.
My hands cleared up totally and I can toss my high fiber laxatives.

My hands are so clear, I can even wash dishes (and my hair)
without gloves. Plus I lost the excess weight I'd gained after three
pregnancies and a sluggish system improved greatly.

> *Mrs. L. Floreen*
> *New Westminster, B.C*

We have taken a quick trip through the body and seen some of the
things that can go wrong with it. The many different types of diseases can't be covered even in an extensive pathology course. The
important thing to remember is that the body wants to heal itself
and will do so if the obstacles to cure are removed. There is only one
major hurdle to overcome. As that wise Pogo once said, "I have seen
the enemy and it is us."

In the next section we will turn your worst enemy back into a
good friend by learning how to "tune up your digestive system".

PART II

EATING ALIVE:

"Good dyet is a perfect way of curing:
And worthy much regard and health assuring.
A king that cannot rule him in his dyet,
Will hardly rule his Realme in peace and quiet."
Regimen Sanitis Salernitanum, 11th Century.

CHAPTER 5

Is Disease a Mystery?

There are people who think that to be healthy they must be healed. Doctors, drugs, vitamins, healers, surgery, magic chants, diets, incantations, painful postures, absolutions, strenuous exertions, exotic herbs and expensive potions have been developed to fulfill this need.

It may be true that these will help. It is also true that the body knows how to heal itself. In fact, except for a few genetic and developmental defects, the body knows how to take perfect care of itself.

It is known from research that cells can be kept alive beyond life expectancy with a steady flow of nutrients and, equally important, quick removal of wastes. Cells thrive when given these two conditions: nutrients and elimination of toxins.

Homeostasis is the ability of the body to regulate its cells together as a unit. The body knows just where it should be going and just how to get there.

Isn't it remarkable that everyone in the world has a little internal elf that is flipping switches and turning valves so as to keep the body's temperature at 98.6 degrees F.!

Just think, whether a Bedouin in the sweltering desert or an Eskimo in the freezing Arctic, the body is effortlessly making billions of biochemical adjustments to maintain its equilibrium. Through the most phenomenal of physical stresses this internal intelligence is constantly measuring and balancing, juggling and adapting, always aiming for those common pre-set goals. All of this goes on despite differences of race, sex, nationality, financial status, or political or religious belief.

All who study the body closely must recognize it as living magic.

The following quote is by Nobel Prize winner Dr. Albert Szent-Gyorgyi:

"As a medical student, I learned about those thousand diseases humanity is suffering from. . . . Since then, as a biochemist, I am living in silent admiration of the wonderful precision, adaptability and perfection of our body. Medicine taught me the shocking imperfection, biochemistry the wonderful perfection, and I have wondered where the contradiction lies. Anything that Nature produces seems to be perfect. Should, then, man be the only imperfect creature kept alive in the face of all his imperfections only by means created by his own mind?"

The body can withstand a phenomenal amount of abuse, and homeostasis will maintain internal equilibrium without us even being aware of the process. If homeostasis is pushed harder to maintain order then acute disease exists. High fever helps the white blood cells to be more active. Vomiting and diarrhea can help to flush out toxins. Lack of appetite allows the body to focus on cleansing and repair instead of digestion. Fatigue allows the body energy to be shunted away from motion, inwards to aid healing. Acute disease should quickly and decisively re-establish homeostasis.

If it is unsuccessful in achieving its goals due to a healing capacity that is lower than the disease cause, then the body will slowly surrender its idealistic goals. This is the beginning of chronic disease.

The classical causes of disease such as plague, famine and exposure to the environment have little relevance in modern society, at least in the First World. Medicine has been befuddled by degenerative disease over the last hundred and fifty years or so, and is constantly waiting for future research breakthroughs to shed light on the darkness of disease. In the meantime, patients are "practised" on.

Not everyone has been so reticent to voice an opinion as to disease cause. The following is from Natural Therapeutics, Vol. 3, "Dietetics" by Henry Lindlahr, published in 1914:

"... Practically all disease arising in the human organism is caused originally by the accumulation of these effete waste and end-products of digestion and of the tissue changes."

In a similar vain, Thomas Sydenham, the famous seventeenth century English physician, summed up disease with this statement:

"Disease is nothing else but an attempt on the part of the body to rid itself of morbific matter."

In his book "The Wheel of Health" Dr. G.T. Wrench wrote:

"Diseases only attack those whose outer circumstances, particularly food, are faulty... The prevention and banishment of disease are primarily matters of food; secondarily, of suitable conditions of environment. Antiseptics, medicaments, inoculations, and extirpating operations evade the real problem. Disease is the censor pointing out the humans, animals and plants who are imperfectly nourished."

The "Father of Cellular Pathology", Rudolph Virchow stated:
"If I could live my life over again I would devote it to proving
that germs seek their natural habitat-diseased tissue-rather
than being the cause of diseased tissue.... "

It is rumoured that even the Master of the Microbe himself, Louis
Pasteur, had a major change of thought on his deathbed and stated
that the resistance of the individual is more important than germs in
the causation of disease.

Chronic disease is simply the inability of acute reactions to
reestablish homeostasis.

Chronic diseases are those little or big complaints that refuse to go
away on their own, no matter how patient you are or how hard you
wish. The important thing to remember is that, except for genetic
problems, your body wants to return to its normal state. Since the
blood is the body's healing agent, where chronic disease exists there
must be "weak blood". Since blood is a product of diet, digestion and
assimilation, these must be improved. Simply improving diet is usually not enough to reverse chronic disease.

The emphasis in this book, as it is my practice, is not on what I
can do for you, but on what you can do for yourself. The word Doc-

tor comes from the latin "To Teach". In Part I we learned that disease is a gradual process beginning in early childhood with physical aggravation of the stomach, which eventually leads to decreased absorption of nutrients and increased formation of toxins that can overload the liver/gallbladder and lymphatic system. Since cells need nutrients rather than toxins to run properly, improving health is simply a matter of improving the nutrient content of the blood and at the same time decreasing the toxins.

Since nutrients get into the blood by proper diet, digestion and absorption, and excess toxins occur due to improper diet, digestion, absorption and elimination. If you can improve diet, digestion, absorption and elimination, then you will both increase nutrients in the blood and decrease toxins. If this increased blood quality is strong enough and maintained long enough, then it may be possible to reverse even chronic disease.

Thus, proper DIET + strong DIGESTION + complete ABSORPTION = STRONG BLOOD + Complete CIRCULATION + Efficient ELIMINATION = GOOD HEALTH.

Your body knows how to heal itself and wants to do it now. Have faith in it but also supply it with the proper physical tools.

PATIENT'S LETTER

Most of my thirty-two years of life have been spent suffering from a variety of "undiagnosed" illnesses. These included digestive problems, gallbladder disorders, chronic colds and sore throats, nerve-related dysfunction, headaches, PMS and for the last year-severe diarrhea and increased weight gain. After visiting countless G.P.s and specialists over the years (four of them alone in the six months prior to Dr. Matsen) not one of them was able to find a "medical" reason for my problems.

After hearing of Dr. Matsen's philosophy and treatment I decided to give it a chance. After four months of his program I am happy to say that I have lost twenty-seven pounds (my desired weight loss) and the diarrhea has long since disappeared!! As well, all the other symptoms that plagued me are long gone as well. I FEEL MARVELOUS! I have much more energy along with a great sense of well-being. Thank you Dr. Matsen for changing my health through my eating habits.

> *Maureen Fairfax*
> *Surrey, B.C.*

CHAPTER 6

Diet

Let's begin with DIET. The goal of diet should be to provide all the essential nutrients without aggravating the function of the digestive organs.

Since we have found the stomach of almost everyone over the age of two (and sometimes younger) to be in a state of "shock", the thing to do is to remove the irritants so that the stomach muscle can "de-spasm" and regain proper function.

The reason many people don't get improved stomach function from improved diet is that they haven't eliminated everything that aggravates the digestive organs.

Consider the stomach as being like a young child who has been beaten ruthlessly since birth. It's been hiding in the attic, occasionally whimpering, as you continued to torment it.

So now we've learned the error of our ways and we're going to stop mistreating this sensitive little thing so that it can come down out of hiding and resume useful function. During the first few weeks it's going to still be highly sensitive and the slightest abuse will send it scuttering into spasm again, so care must be taken to avoid every single thing that bothers it. Once it's been fully in operation for a while and is less sensitive, you may give it a little friendly smack once in a while without it going back into complete shock.

In practise I test every person on approximately one hundred things using applied kinesiology (muscle testing) to see what is good and bad for their stomachs. If such testing isn't available to you, there are several general patterns that have shown up after using various testing methods on thousands of patients. Before describing these, I will repeat that a person with a major health problem still must seek out professional guidance, as there are many obstacles to cure in severe chronic disease.

Since some things show up as problems for virtually every person, it can only be assumed that these are not foods. Let's call this . . .

GROUP I. It includes coffee, tea, chocolate, white sugar, alcohol, artificial sweeteners and preservatives and salt and tobacco. It takes little awareness to realize that the effect of most of these is as stimulants, not nutrients. They are used to whip an overloaded liver and/or stressed adrenals into one more round of struggle. Unfortunately their end result is to cause further weakness of these organs as well as thoroughly irritating the stomach.

This is not new information, but it is still largely ignored by the majority of people. It goes without saying that it has only been in the last few years that tobacco has been recognized by western medicine as toxic, in spite of alternative practitioners speaking against it for over a hundred years. The fact that smoking is still increasing in some segments of society only shows our slowness to accept even the obvious. Many of us need to experience the full brunt of major disease before we will accept the need for change. Since disease is really a warning from the body that change is necessary, I find it is more beneficial to encourage some people to eat and drink to excess than to discourage them. Many people need to get to the physical breaking point before they become motivated to make changes.

I find it interesting that when the stomach, intestine, liver/gallbladder and adrenals have fully recovered from the use of stimulants, there is much more energy than that false energy given by the stimulants. Without eliminating Group I for at least three weeks it

will be virtually impossible to get the stomach "deshocked" and back to work making digestive juices and "sparking" the intestinal tract back to life. Perhaps the one exception to that is tobacco. Tobacco does have a negative effect on the stomach but its worst effects are on the lungs, liver and arteries. It is usually possible to get the stomach back to work without quitting smoking, though the lungs won't recover until smoking stops.

GROUP II. Baking yeast, peanuts, brown sugar, cow products and pork also show up for almost everyone.

GROUP III contains wheat, tomatoes, brewer's yeast and mushrooms which show up frequently.

GROUP IV contains other things sometimes seen as problems, such as lamb, beef, chicken, turkey, eggs, shellfish, fish, soya, lemon, oranges, grapefruit, pineapple, apples, bananas, peaches, currants, raisins, apricots, strawberries, potatoes, squash, rye, oats, rice, corn, alfalfa, eggplant, carrots, cabbage, broccoli, cauliflower, celery, cucumbers, peppers, turnips, walnuts, cashews, brazil nuts, honey, maple syrup, molasses, raw sugar, curry, garlic, vinegar and onions.

One reason why most diets don't actually improve the function of the stomach is that every single thing that irritates the stomach must be eliminated.

If we go back to what we learned in Part I, there are three ways that the stomach can be physically irritated.

The first way is by putting into it things that aggravate it. Everyone's stomach is aggravated by the items in Group I. Group II usually should be avoided as well for a time. A person with any signs or symptoms of disease should also avoid Group III for a few weeks. A person with major disease should be tested to see if any items in Group IV cause problems.

The second way that the stomach can get irritated is from toxins spilling past the liver into the main bloodstream so that every cell in the body is irritated and thus sensitized. This also makes the stomach more sensitive to foods. The goal is to decrease these toxins by speeding up your digestion, slowing down the digestion of the "critters" and improving liver function.

The third way the stomach can be irritated is by toxic bile from the gallbladder being dumped into the base of the stomach (duodenum) which can dramatically cause stomach, esophagus and intestinal spasm and discomfort. Most people who complain of digestive symptoms are actually experiencing them from toxic bile irritation, as the "shocked" stomach that we find almost everyone has since childhood usually is "silent" or symptom free.

To decrease this irritation the bile must be made less toxic by speeding up digestion, slowing down the unfavourable flora and improving liver/gallbladder function. The function of the ileocecal valve is of extreme importance for this, and I must repeat that at least half of the patients I see who are on self-imposed diets have aggravated this valve.

Usually the stomach will spontaneously "de-shock" itself after a period of time without aggravation, and begin to function again. This time period may be anywhere from a few days to a few months. Generally we allow three weeks for the stomach to begin to function properly again.

A person who is in reasonably good health should be able to get the stomach working by avoiding everything listed in GROUPS I, II and III for three to eight weeks, by which time all the digestive organs should be functioning well enough to add back II and III if the other steps outlined are followed diligently. The items listed in the first group are permanently a problem, though once the organs are detoxified and functioning at their best a person may be able to withstand a little occasional abuse.

After about three weeks the foods in GROUPS IV and III become less of a problem as the body detoxifies, and there is usually little problem with them being added back. Anyone with a particular problem should be retested at this point to make sure that improvement is occurring before these two groups are added back.

PATIENTS' LETTERS

I am a sixty-nine year old lady who had been suffering from abdominal pains, periods of great physical weakness, lack of energy and, most distressing, periods of confusion. As I have always been very energetic and clear-headed I found this quite depressing. For some time I had not been driving my car for fear of making mistakes in traffic or of getting lost.

By the time I made my first appointment with Dr. Matsen, I had already seen my regular Medical Doctor and specialists, none of whom could find anything wrong with me. I required my son to accompany me on the bus for my appointments with Dr. Matsen, again because I feared getting confused and lost on my way there.

Dr. Matsen performed several tests and prescribed a diet and naturopathic medicines. I found this difficult because I could not eat many of the foods I have eaten all my life, but I persevered.

Although it took some time, I slowly noticed that my periods of weakness and confusion became fewer and less severe. After several months of treatment I find that although I am not as well as I would like to be, I am very much better than before. I have dared to drive my car around the block a few times, take the bus to go shopping and can again tolerate (within moderation) many of the foods I have missed.

Mrs. K. Hamadan
Vancouver, B.C.

I first saw Dr. Matsen in July of 1984 after giving up on conventional medicine regarding my physical condition. I had chronic indigestion, constant pain and discomfort and a very low energy level. Dr. Matsen after carefully listening to what I had to say and making the tests required, put me on a diet and gave me some supplements. I followed the diet for 6 months very accurately and began to notice changes in the first week. Very soon my energy level changed in such a way that I can honestly say I feel better than I did 10 years ago.

After six months, I did make the occasional mistake with my eating habits, with no negative results at all. Two years have gone by now. I have never again had any problem with my digestive system. Headaches that I thought were related to a previous brain surgery have disappeared as well.

I have just returned from a trip to Europe where for 3 weeks I kept no diet at all and I was amazed to realize that my system did not react in any negative way. The reinforcement that my "special diet" provided me with on the trip encouraged me to go back to the strict diet in order to cleanse myself from what I basically consider "junk food" and food combinations.

I am deeply thankful to Dr. Matsen for my well-being and I have referred many other patients to him and will continue to do so.

> *Yours truly,*
> *Marianne Haebler*
> *Vancouver, B.C*

CHAPTER 7

Digestion

The ultimate truth out of all this is that it isn't the foods at all that are the problem. The real problem is with the digestive vitality of the person.

Think of the digestive system as resembling a flame. If you have a tiny flame then you have to treat it with great care. The fuel must be pure and fine and added slowly, or the fire will flicker and possibly falter.

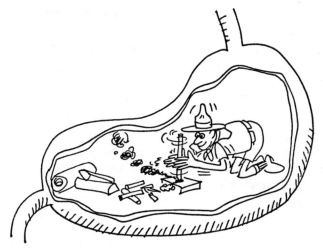

However, if you gradually build up that little flame so that it reaches bonfire proportions, then you can throw the occasional wet log or large chunk on it with only a little smoke being produced. However, many people are busily throwing wet logs on their digestive candles and wondering why their bodies are getting "sooted up".

The confusion over diet is mainly because changing diet by itself doesn't usually improve digestion, so a person remains highly sensitive to many different foods. Sensitivities, or allergies to foods or external substances like pollen or dust, decrease if the digestion is improved and toxins eliminated. If a person can increase digestive vitality, the dietary range can also be increased.

There is no doubt that a person with a strong genetic constitution, healthy intestinal flora (not ravaged by western medicine) and a digestion free from the worries and troubles of life, can eat and drink with abandon for a considerable period of time. However, the prevalence of chronic disease (physical, mental and emotional) in our society indicates that eventually there are limits. However, contrary to what some diet books claim, it's not necessary to be a vegetarian to be healthy. It's also not necessary to eat meat. What is important is that you digest quickly and efficiently whatever you eat.

There is a certain macho nobility to this concept that nutrition is basically a blank cheque. Free of petty restraints, man challenges himself with gluttony: A duel of digestion versus indulgence.

Unfortunately, the only crossed swords in this duel are the scalpels of the surgeons as they remove the gallbladder, uterus, intestine or other casualties. Even the strongest constitution has weak links that must eventually show the strain.

As medicine has gradually assumed responsibility for human health over the last hundred years and disease has become a more and more complex mystery that only big-buck research money can unravel, the stampede to junk food and artificial additives has been allowed to proceed uninhibited, and has perhaps even been encouraged by Big Medicine. Perhaps the ultimate irony is when junk-food franchises sponsor homes for sick children. Is this a conscious or unconscious attempt to ease guilt feelings?

Specific testing that has evolved in the last few decades has helped overcome the confusion that has prevailed around diet. Testing indicates that most people these days have weak digestion and poor intestinal flora, especially children.

Junk food not only feeds the critters their favourite delicacies, but also irritates the digestive organs and reduces digestive speed and efficiency, which of course further aids the intestinal festivities.

Most children show an accumulation of metabolic debris that sensitizes the body. They show reactions to many foods. Any particular food can become a problem as the breakdown of the digestive process and elimination organs continues. While there are certain foods that show up often as problems, anything can show up. Allergies represent only one type of reaction the body can have against specific foods. There are other types that can be lumped together under the general category of food sensitivities.

If people simply stay away from those foods, they may start to feel a little better for a while. However, if the digestive process isn't improved they will eventually develop senstivities to other foods. If they eat in a way that eases the strain on the digestive organs, such as food combining, they will get even better results. However, if they also actually rebuild the digestive organ function, they will slowly detoxify and desensitize the body to the point that the individual foods are no longer a problem. The need for some of the food combinations may disappear as well. As the toxins decrease, external allergies fade away. Aches and pains, fatigue, skin problems, moodiness etc. may disappear as well.

The result of digestive strength is dietary freedom. This is best expressed in the last patient's letter of Chapter 6, as it expresses the ultimate goal of this book. That is to get you so HEALTHY that you have complete freedom to live as you want, but to have you AWARE enough to realize that your health depends on the strength of your digestive system, and to have you MOTIVATED enough that you will WANT to guard this precious resource, and to have you EDUCATED enough so that you will know how to look after it.

Avoiding specific food sensitivities is the first step to rebuilding back the digestive system. The next step is avoiding combinations of foods that are problems.

Mixing certain foods together causes health problems because carbohydrates are first digested by alkaline juices from the mouth, and proteins are digested by acid juices from the stomach. Eating the two foods together results in neutralization of the digestive juices so that the food takes much longer to digest.

Since the digestive time is extended the chances of fermentation and putrefaction toxins being formed by the intestinal flora is increased proportionately. Since there is a race between you and the "Bad Guys" to digest your food, you need all the help you can get.

Separating proteins and carbohydrates from each other allows the mouth and stomach to participate more fully in digestion, thus speeding up digestion and also making it more efficient.

Testing indicates that food combination problems vary from person to person, but as in testing individual food sensitivities, there are certain common patterns that emerge.

In the same way that specific food sensitivities are considered temporary, so are some of the food combinations. Improving function of the digestive organs will decrease the need for certain combinations, as we will learn later. However, on testing over five thousand patients from birth to old age, I have found that nearly everyone who's been off mother's milk for over a year shows weakness of the digestive organs and needs to separate certain foods from each other when eating.

Carbohydrates and proteins should not be eaten together. Anyone who's read Fit For Life will be aware of this. While this need isn't recognized by conventional nutrition, I concur completely with the Diamonds on this. Mixing carbohydrates and proteins together in the average person causes increased toxicity.

The sweeter and the more refined the carbohydrate, such as white sugar, the more it inhibits the digestion of proteins. The heavier the protein, such as red meat, the longer it takes to digest and the more its digestion can be inhibited by carbohydrates.

Proteins are most notable for the nitrogen groups that they contain. The vegetable proteins may take three to four hours to digest, while the animal proteins may take up to six hours. These numbers are extremely speculative; there are many other factors that affect digestion.

Carbohydrates are all made of sugars joined together. The tighter the bond, such as in starches, the less sweetness can be tasted. Holding a starch in the mouth for a short time allows the enzymes of the saliva to break the sugar bonds, and it starts to taste sweet.

A piece of fruit may take an hour to digest. A rice and bean meal may take three to four hours or longer.

Mixing the two groups together greatly increases the production of intestinal toxins in most people, by neutralizing the production of digestive juice and giving the intestinal flora more time to go back for seconds in the intestinal smorgasbord. Their waste products (toxins) are what then foul up the elimination organs and cause most disease.

The sweeter and more refined the carbohydrate, the more it interferes with stomach acid, so whoever invented dessert was way off the mark. The continued use of sweets, even fruit, after protein is the worst of the combinations, and is one of the most destructive to health. This can also be said of most fruit juices combined with protein meals.

Separating the two food groups leads to simpler, quicker, more complete digestion and less party time for the guys downstairs. Less toxin production means more opportunity for your body to absorb nutrients, eliminate cell wastes and maintain homeostasis.

Some books claim that these combinations are rigid, but that's not what I find in practise. For example, there is an exception to this rule for people who are hypermetabolic. These are people who burn up calories extremely quickly. They are very lean, sometimes gaunt if suffering from absorption problems. Testing indicates they will do better mixing proteins and starches or grains together. This helps to slow down their high metabolic rate.

I look at food combining principles more as stepping-stones to improve the function of the digestive organs than as absolute rules. When the digestive organs have regained proper functioning and the intestinal flora are properly reestablished the need for some of these combinations lessens for many people. So there is an option period down the road where you can decide whether to stick to the stricter diet or make additions as improvement in health is made. It is important to follow the stricter diet as closely as possible at the beginning.

The purpose of food combining is to speed up digestion to the point that the intestinal flora have little time to produce new toxins. If digestion can be made so efficient that extra digestive energy is left over, that's what is sent out into the bloodstream to clean out the old accumulated toxins. Thus it's our surplus digestive energy that does the housecleaning in the body.

Since most of us have such overloaded digestive systems, we do little in the way of housecleaning over the years, which is the equivalent of living in a house for many years without vaccuuming it. It's bound to get a little dusty in the corners eventually.

Our ancestors did internal housecleaning whether they wanted to or not, because a hundred years or more ago they were mainly a bunch of starving peasants. They had certain natural advantages over us. Their food was wholesome and natural, their intestinal flora were most likely healthy, and most important, they ran out of food often. In other words they got hungry. When you're hungry your digestive energy goes out into the blood looking for fuel. It starts to digest your body to meet its requirements for energy. Fortunately, at the beginning, it begins to digest a lot of the old debris lying around. So being a little bit hungry actually worked to their advantage by allowing the digestive energy to do a little housecleaning. Of course being too hungry too long eventually leads to starvation and death, but our ancestors never succumbed to this dire fate or we wouldn't be here talking about them.

Thousands of years ago one of those peasants must have realized that he or she felt a lot better during one of those hungry periods, and even when food became abundant again he went without eating occasionally to recapture that good feeling. Thus fasting was discovered.

Fasting became an important part of every culture. Since people tended to not only become more physically healthy as they detoxified but they also felt better mentally, emotionally and spiritually during fasting, it was built into the rituals and traditions of all the religions.

Most people today are so toxic that fasting stirs old toxins up far faster than their already-overloaded elimination organs can handle. Feeling worse is often the result. Once the fast is over, they're also still stuck with the same old run-down digestive system that's going to just go on dumping more and more fresh toxins into the system.

The good news is that you can now get all of the benefits of fasting WHILE YOU'RE STILL EATING.

If your digestion is very efficient, you have surplus digestive juice left over to go out into the blood to do your housecleaning. While our ancestors fasted frequently to accomplish improved health, with the understanding you will get from this book you will be able to get all the benefits of fasting while you're still eating.

The digestive system has highs and lows of energy, as do all the organs of the body. The Chinese have observed these energy flows carefully for thousands of years and have produced a very accurate clock which depicts the times of strength and weakness of the different organs.

The digestive system is strongest between seven and eleven in the morning. The stomach meridian's peak is between seven and nine, and that of the pancreas (spleen meridian) is between nine and eleven. This is the time to eat a big breakfast like the nutritionists have been harping at us to do for such a long time. People who do heavy physical labour such as loggers, construction workers, farmers, and ranchers etc. are famous for their enormous breakfasts.

The problem with eating a big breakfast is, however, that all the prime digestive juice is used up first thing in the morning, so it's virtually impossible to have any surplus digestive juice left for the rest of the day. No housecleaning will be done that day, and if a massive breakfast isn't burnt off by heavy labour (and how many people eat as if they were going to work hard and then they go and sit at a machine or in an office all day?) then that mass of food is going to feed the harmful flora and end up dumping more toxins into the system. Not only is no housecleaning done, but more metabolic debris accumulates.

To get housecleaning done you have to avoid a big breakfast. Well, a lot of people say, "I never eat breakfast so I must be doing housecleaning every morning." Then you find out they run on coffee or tea or chocolate or sugar all morning. Remember, these are all

Group I foods, which means they are all direct irritants to virtually everyone's stomach. So the stomach is so aggravated that it will be tightened up and not make proper digestive juice, and the person will be even worse off. No, there will be no housecleaning done that day either. In fact the liver is going to be even more overloaded, trying to break down the toxins found in these non-foods.

To do housecleaning you have to trick the body in the morning, to make more digestive juice than is actually needed.

This surplus digestive juice will head out into the bloodstream where it will start to clean up a lot of the old debris lying around.

We need something in the morning that will stimulate the production of digestive juice, but it has to be something light that doesn't require much digestion itself. Fruit or vegetable juice or broth are the things that will accomplish this.

Probably the most effective thing that I have found is a variation of the Master Cleanser fasting drink. Squeeze a little fresh lemon (approximately two tablespoons) into a glass of hot water. Add a pinch of cayenne, and a little ginger if you like. The ingredients and proportions can be varied to suit individual taste. If sweetener is necessary add a little maple syrup, honey or molasses.

Lemon, cayenne and ginger are all mild stomach stimulants, so they will stimulate the stomach to make lots of digestive juice. However there is little in this drink that requires digestion, so considerable surplus digestive energy is produced. This goes out into the blood and starts to "vacuum" out the far corners of the body.

Grapefruit or any of the other acid group can be substituted, especially if weight-loss is required. Apple cider vinegar in water is sometimes beneficial, especially in cases of arthritis. Acids before proteins can aid their digestion.

Since we do specific food testing before we work out a diet, we occasionally find that lemon or the other acids aggravate some people. In this case the other fruits might be used. Kiwi, papaya and pineapple are good, due to their protein-digesting enzymes.

Cooking and canning papaya and pineapple neutralizes their enzymes. Raw pineapple enzymes can be irritating to some people. Sub-acid fruits can stimulate surplus digestive juices, though less so than the acids.

The sweet fruits are best used fresh and whole. Juicing and drying tends to amplify their sweetness. Since the sweeter and more refined something is the quicker intestinal yeast can turn it into toxins, it is better to avoid excess sweets.

The fruits should also be used by themselves at this point, so that they don't act as primer for the yeast to ferment starches and grains. You know that if you're baking bread and you mix yeast and flour together nothing happens.

If you want to get the bread to rise, you first must add a little sweetener to the yeast to get it started. As the yeast becomes active it can take the starch of the flour as fuel. The same general thing happens when you mix fruit and grains together. The yeast starts on the fruit and becomes so active that it can then take the grains as well.

Grapes are probably the closest to being perfect fruits as readily-available energy, and they rarely show problems on testing.

However, sometimes all the fruits test as a problem. Then what is recommended first thing in the morning is vegetable juice or broth.

Fresh vegetable juice is preferable. Carrot, celery, beet (usually an ounce or two added to other juices) or cabbage are the most commonly used. Other juiceable vegetables are radish, cucumber, lettuce, garlic, onion, brussels sprouts, asparagus, potatoes and greens. The juices of the common forage plants such as alfalfa, wheat grass and barley grass are extremely important for the severe chronic degenerative diseases, and some day they will probably be as commonplace in stores as milk and bread. For further information on vegetable juices see Norman Walker's book, "Fresh Juices".

Yeast, even when living inside the body like mold, fungi and mushrooms, is much more active in cold wet weather.

This is why some people with asthma or arthritis feel much better when they move to Arizona. In effect, the yeast "dries up" and is less active. The reverse holds true as well. I see many patients who lived happily and healthily in Africa, South America and India but after a winter or two of cold wet Vancouver weather they may suffer from innumerable complaints.

They are told that it's the stress of moving to a new culture that is the problem, but often we find by improving diet, digestion and absorption they feel much better. Often they are on very high carbohydrate diets which are quite suitable for warm climates but which end up feeding yeast during the cold wet winters.

Old Mother Nature obviously had this all figured out, so she made fruit ripe in hot, dry weather. The hotter and drier the weather, the sweeter the fruit. By making sweet fruit ripe at the time the intestinal yeast is least active, she helps you get full benefit from eating fruit. By eating sweet fruit in the winter, we end up feeding the yeast if it is a major portion of the intestinal flora. Of course in extreme cases yeast can even digest fruit in the summer, even if eaten alone. In these cases fruit must be avoided completely until the intestinal critters can be controlled.

If acceptable, we usually recommend fruit first thing, especially the lemon drink in colder climates. The lemon drink and other fruits can be repeated as often as wanted in the morning. Fruit is readily digested and will leave a surplus of digestive juice left over for housecleaning.

However, fruit "stirs up the old toxins" so we don't want to go on fruit all day. There might be more stirred up than your elimination organs can handle.

Since the high mineral content of vegetable juice or broth tends to buffer or neutralize toxins, they would follow fruit very well an hour or two after. The high mineral content also seems to stimulate the body to heal the now-detoxified area.

So we might have fruit in the morning, possibly followed by vegetable juice or broth. Then we want to get a little hungry before we actually eat. It's okay to get a little hungry; that's your body burning up some of the old junk for fuel, like a mini-fast. However, it's important to take it very easy in the early stages. The liver is the major organ for regulating blood-sugar levels. Most people's livers are fouled up with years of toxic accumulation and don't handle blood sugar very well. If you go too long without eating at this point you may experience low blood-sugar symptoms. Since it is the brain that needs blood sugar most, the symptoms may include light-headedness, weakness, confusion. It feels like a curtain of fog descending over the brain. Usually eating quickly relieves the symptoms, but sometimes it takes a little time to get over the symptoms.

The earlier nutritionists used to tell people to carry sugar cubes with them, as sucking on them would quickly raise the blood-sugar levels. This certainly works in the short term but it tends to worsen the problem in the long run, as the refined sugar is released too quickly and the body creates an even stronger rebound effect against this sudden increase in blood sugar.

The newer approach is to eat heavy foods such as proteins, fats or starches often, so that the gradual release of sugar from these slow-digesting foods will slowly raise the blood-sugar level. This approach is more effective at balancing the blood sugar levels, but unfortunately doesn't leave any time when your digestive system is not loaded down with food, and thus eliminates any possibility of detoxification and prevents the possibility of actually curing the problem.

To cure hypoglycemia, the organs have to be detoxified to regain the proper regulation of blood sugar levels. It is therefore important to eat lightly in the morning in order to send surplus digestive juice into the bloodstream, but not so light so long that you actually get low blood-sugar symptoms.

Since this is an individual matter we don't tell anyone to go any particular length of time before actually eating. Ideally one should stay on fruit and/or vegetable juice till eleven or twelve or even one o'clock, but if a person can only go for an hour or two, that's fine.

That hour or two of detoxification might allow the liver to slowly function a little better by the next day, week or month.

People who are younger, weaker or more hypermetabolic, doing heavier work, or experiencing the colder seasons should shorten the time they will go light in the morning.

When one does eat, it's important to avoid mixing the carbohydrates and proteins so as to speed up the digestion and thus reduce the feeding time of the harmful flora. Usually the lunch meal is from the carbohydrate side rather than the protein side, as carbohydrates are clean-burning. When burnt for fuel, the end products are water and carbon dioxide, which are easily eliminated. Protein can also be burnt for fuel, but its nitrogen has to first be stripped off, and it then becomes another burden on the elimination organs.

If the protein is eaten at the end of the day it is more likely that the protein will be used as building material, which is its most important use rather than being burnt up as fuel.

However, there are situations where it is easier or more advisable to have protein at lunch, and that's fine.

No matter whether carbohydrates or protein are used at lunch, the protective foods which are neutral can be used with either. They buffer against putrefaction and fermentation of either proteins or carbohydrates.

Neutrals can be used alone if one doesn't need a high caloric intake. This woudn't be advisable at the start for someone with hypoglycemic tendencies.

Fruit might take an hour to digest, so nothing else should be taken in during that period. A light starch meal such as a muffin might take two to three hours, and again, nothing else should be taken during that time. A heavy carbohydrate meal like rice and beans might take three to five hours to digest.

The lighter proteins like tofu might take three hours, dairy products three to four, fish and poultry four to five, red meats five and pork six hours. Of course these times are purely speculative and can vary with a number of factors, and are given as a general guideline as to how much time to leave between meals.

What we have discussed here is the basic premise of Fit For Life, that not mixing certain foods makes food more rapidly digested and causing less toxins to be formed in the intestinal tract, enabling the body to function better The newer energy-testing techniques verify

what many alternative practitioners have been saying for decades: that separating food groups aids health.

If this agrees with Fit For Life, why should we have another book that says basically the same thing?

Well, there's a little more to it than that. While the new testing verifies the philosophy of food combinations, there is other testing that shows that dietary changes alone don't usually make a big enough improvement in digestive function to reverse chronic disease consistently. Also when corrections are made to improve digestion, then the need for the stricter food combining is reduced.

PATIENTS' LETTERS

Naturopathic medicine is curative medicine, preventative medicine and family medicine.

We have five children now aged four to twelve and they have all suffered from repeated ear infections and strep throat. They received repeated doses of antibiotics and in October of 1984 alone I spent one hundred dollars in antibiotics that never seemed to work for long. The specialist wanted to have tubes put in the ears of Stephanie. Instead I went to Dr. Matsen and by avoiding certain foods and following food combining we are now down to maybe one infecton per year. I took Stephanie back to the specialist and he now says that her ears are fine. Now their bodies are strong enough to fight infections on their own. By going to a naturopath I saved our family a lot of stress and also saved our medical plan a lot of money that would have gone to repeated visits to specialists.

> *Sincerely,*
> *Illene Pevec*
> *North Vancouver, B.C.*

My wife Joan had been bothered by hot flushes and heart arrhythmia. After starting on your diet she began to lose weight, she felt more energetic and the above problems disappeared. An additional bonus was that her menstrual cycle also stabilized.

My eldest son Julian, who had lived away from home on a poor diet, lost quite a lot of hair, certainly more than would be expected in a twenty year old male. After some time on your recommended diet and supplements his hair regrew in almost all its previous areas.

My second son Adam had been a keen long distance runner with apparently inexhaustible energy. However, three different antibiotics prescribed for him in response to a tooth extraction infection appeared to upset his body chemistry. For almost two years he was very lethargic. In recent times he had to sleep for an hour after a seven hour day's work. After your prescribed diet and supplements he has recovered much of his previous energy and I'm glad to be able to report he is running long distances again.

Because it involved my own body my personal experience was the most striking. I had suffered from migraine headaches for many years. In recent months these became more frequent, e.g. five in the first month of this year, each one lasting two to three days during which I was unable to attend work. I have been to regular doctors and specialists who have assured me that there was nothing seriously wrong but could do no more than recommend avoidance of triggers and prescribe medication to dull the severity of the attacks.

After only three days on your diet and supplements I started to feel better. I awoke each morning with far more energy than I have been used to for years. I lost about eight pounds in body weight and still feel much better for that. But the most significant result for me is that since I started the diet I have not had one minor headache. It feels so good to be out of that recurring cycle of tension and migraine that I had come to expect as unavoidable. In addition, my brain seems to work much better. I am able to remember details and peoples' names much better than I have ever done in the last ten years. To sum it all up, I feel great.

My family and I want to express our gratitude to you for this marked improvement in our health. It worked just as you said it would and we are very grateful to you.

Malcolm K. Smith
North Vancouver, B.C.

CHAPTER 8

Absorption and Detoxification

Getting the stomach working again is an important step towards health. However, getting the intestine working properly is the next step.

More importantly, a very large percentage of people I see who have been following diets have actually worsened their health. I call this "Health Book Syndrome", because usually the worse the blood picture, the more health books the person has read.

There were several events that really opened my eyes to the prevalence and potential seriousness of overdoing anything, even something as apparently innocuous as diet. There was a big strong young construction labourer whom I had started treating. After a few visits to set up a diet for him, he didn't return. Often patients wish to take a slower pace than the one we set out for them, so I never thought anything of it. Several months later he came in and I could hardly recognize him. He was weak, emaciated, physically and emotionally exhausted. He had started on my diet, but had met a local raw-foods advocate who told him to throw away our program and she would have him really healthy in no time. She put him on a rigorous raw-foods diet without any personalized testing. He immediately felt worse and began to lose weight rapidly. Her explanation was that he was detoxifying and would soon feel better. When his physical decline continued and emotional weakness started, she said that the only place that could help him was in Texas. At great expense to him, he flew to Texas where the treatment was continued and his decline went on unabated.

When he finally came in to see me again, his metabolism had become so hyper from his weakened state that he actually tested stronger on mixing carbohydrates and proteins together. Also, he had been given a lot of fruit which he was sensitive to. He also had a severe intestinal flora imbalance which wasn't dealt with. They had eliminated protein from his diet, which was something he had a higher-than-average need for. Most importantly, he was given too much scratchy fiber for his intestine to handle, and his ileocecal valve was malfunctioning and dumping large quantities of toxins into the blood. After altering his diet accordingly he regained his physical and emotional strength within a month.

I find that problems with the ileocecal valve have reached almost epidemic proportions and it can be tragic. Shortly after this experience I had two patients within a week who had both been vegetarians for over twenty years, grew much of their own food organically, and practised a certain degree of food combining. One had cancer of the liver, the other hardening of the arteries requiring bypass surgery. It can be a bit intimidating when a patient has already been following the basis of your program, even if without your guidance, and has suffered from it. While they both showed sensitivities to some of the foods they were eating and both showed intestinal flora problems, the major weakness I could identify was an extreme ileocecal valve problem.

Since that time I have checked for ileocecal valve problems much more carefully, and find that nearly half of the people I see for the first time have problems with this important valve. The most common denominator is that almost all of them have actively attempted to improve their health. They have read widely about health and have tried to conscientiously apply what they have read to their day-to-day lifestyle. The other thing in common is that their blood pictures are generally worse than those of people who've never done a thing for their own health.

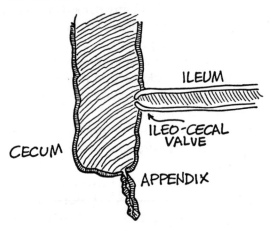

It would appear that health advocates have somehow led people off the road to health. The problem is that fiber is touted as an intestinal broom which can sweep debris from the intestine. Actually the coarser fibers function more as an intestinal rake, irritating the ileocecal valve and thus greatly increasing the quantities of toxins in the blood.

The earlier stages of ileocecal valve problems may not show any signs or symptoms, but as the valve becomes increasingly sensitized a number of things may appear. Probably the most indicative is irregular bowel movements. Every stool may be different. There may be constipation and/or diarrhea. Some of the other indications are tenderness in the lower right abdomen in the area also associated with appendicitis, a sense of fullness after eating small amounts, bloating, and gas. Many of these symptoms may be obviously worse after eating high-fiber foods such as bran or raw vegetables, or irritating spices. The symptoms can be identical to those associated with yeast problems. I find many patients are taking large quanities of yeast killers with little improvement, as the malfunctioning ileocecal valve is the source of their toxicity.

Testing indicates that the main organ to suffer from ileocecal valve problems is the gallbladder, so signs and symptoms may also occur from there.

Poor fat metabolism and the endless list of associated problems, such as acne, hardening of the arteries, strokes and heart attacks, prostaglandin imbalances, weak immunity, stomach spasm and duodenal ulcer from toxic bile irritation, fatigue, and migraines, are sometimes seen with ileocecal problems. Often the person with ileocecal valve problems looks quite healthy, so this barrage of symptoms seems very out of place. It is seldom that anything shows on conventional blood tests, CAT scans, ultrasound or even on physical exam, though a closer look will usually show tenderness deep in the lower right abdomen.

Some patients may have such weakened gallbladder function that they become vegetarians because of their inability to digest fatty foods such as animal proteins. Since many vegetarian diets further emphasize high fiber they can actually make the situation worse. Often a doctor will prescribe more fiber for the bowel problems, or an alternate practitioner will prescribe a raw-food diet, either of which may agrravate the situation. Since the person is now unable to digest the heavier proteins, these are blamed rather than his or her own weakened digestion. I often find the most dogmatic patients have the weakest digestion organs, especially the gallbladder. Sometimes anxiety syndrome is diagnosed, and tranquilizers are prescribed.

To correct an ileocecal valve problem it is important to follow the usual diet and digestion steps: Avoid food sensitivities, especially Group I, do food combinations, avoid scratchy fiber and don't use excessive spice.

Raw vegetables are good for you but it is better to eat the softer things raw, such as leaf lettuce, spinach, avacodoes, sprouts, and tomatoes. The coarser, scratchy vegetables such as celery, broccoli, cauliflower and root vegetables are better juiced if you want them raw, or steamed or otherwise cooked until softened so that their fiber is less irritating.

Grains are dried foods and are quite coarse, irritating to the ileocecal valve. If they are cooked or soaked in water they become softer and less irritating. Oatmeal well-cooked is reasonably soft, while granola is dry and scratchy.

The other way to soften grain fiber is to have it worked over by micro-organisms first. The north European style of making sourdough rye bread by letting bacteria ferment it overnight both softens the fiber and partially predigests the flour, making it easier to digest and preventing any intestinal bad guys from having an easy time on all that fuel. Unfortunately, many sourdough breads these days are made with artificial methods that mimic the action of bacteria but don't have the same beneficial results.

Probably the scratchiest fiber is wheat bran. Baking it, such as in bran muffins, makes it even worse. It's fine if you don't have an ileocecal valve problem, but if you do it has the effect of thousands of little razor blades on a sensitized valve.

If we step back a minute we can see that there is a pattern to this replacement of beneficial creatures. It starts with agriculture.

Fertile soil is a blend of living, dying and dead plants, animals and micro-organisms mixed with the minerals of the earth.

Modern agriculture adds chemicals to boost the minerals available to the plants, and has tried to push the "bad" organisms out of this interdependent environment with pesticides and herbicides.

Similar methods are used in animal husbandry. Antibiotics are considered necessary in the crowded livestock-production environments of today. The residues from those antibiotics and pesticides carry over into the food chain.

Food manufacturing is a major business and its main goal is to get
the food to you before the smaller creatures of the planet get a share
of it and make a profit. The removal of the choicest nutrients in the
food prevents them from getting a crack at it. Of course it also prevents us from getting them. Chemicals are used routinely to prevent
the growth of the opposition.

Medicine has a similar approach: Kill the invaders.

The result of all this applied chemistry has been fantastic. More
food is grown than can possibly be used for years to come. Mine
shafts in the U.S. are filled with wheat and dairy products and
farmers can still grow far more. Stores are filled with a variety and
quantity of food that the rulers of ancient civilizations couldn't have
dreamed of. Hunger is a forgotten word in the mainstream of the in-
dustrialized countries. Infectious disease has been under control for
decades with antibiotics. Things have never looked so good.

Yet you walk down any street in the U.S. and you see that a third
of the population is overweight. Hospitals are overflowing. Patients
are backed up waiting for surgery. The governments of countries
that have taken responsibilty for their citizens' health are approach-

ing bankruptcy trying to maintain free "health" care, but how much has the real health of the population increased? Allergies have become almost normal in North American children while they're unheard of in "underdeveloped" countries.

It takes little insight to realize that the constitutions of our children, which took thousands of generations to build, are rapidly deteriorating due to poor diet and short-sighted medicine. With the same mentality, the soil that is our true wealth, that has taken perhaps tens of thousands of years to build up, is being rapidly depleted.

Is this another of those gloomy stories of impending doom? Certainly not. The human is such a flexible, resilient creature that we will probably stumble through our present crises like we've managed to stumble through all the other troubles of the past. Out of these potential troubles come tremendous opportunities. Farmers have proven that they can grow quantity. The next step is to aim for quality, which also leaves the soil in a richer state. Organic farming has been proven viable. It just requires consumers to ask for quality first.

It may be necessary for more local producers to supply an area, if we want to get quality without all the preservatives.

The depletion of health in many children can be readily reversed, as shown in the letters from patients. The expense of naturopathic medicine is not high. Few of my patients pay over a few hundred dollars for their care at my clinic. Not only did they receive relief of chronic disease that was considered incurable, but they also received a lifelong understanding, as they now know what caused their health problems and what to do to prevent these from returning. Education, not expensive technology, is the key to health.

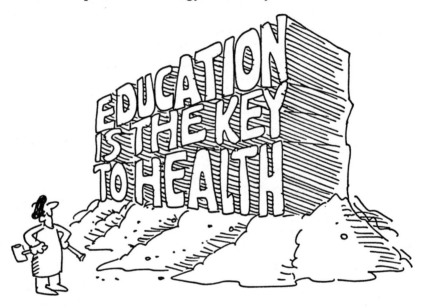

This is not to say there is no place for high-tech medicine. There is not a diagnostic device, drug or surgical technique that doesn't have a time and a place to be used to someone's advantage. Remember though that it is the results of disease that are being dealt with, not the causes.

Since no doctor, type of practise or philosophy of healing can help every patient or every type of problem, it's important that there be a variety of approaches to the treatment of disease. A person who slips through the "safety net" of one mode of healing might still have hope that another practioner with different experiences and insights might catch them and help them back to health.

Naturopathic medicine is time-proven. Its therapies are rooted in antiquity. Hippocrates stated, "Let food be your medicine, and medicine be your food". All cultures have used herbs, hot and cold, fasting and diet to maintain health over thousands of generations. Few of the drugs and surgical methods used in western medicine are over a hundred years old, yet during that period of time naturopathic medicine was almost eliminated.

During the last fifty years, "miracle drugs" and surgical techniques were to rescue helpless humanity forever from the perils of disease. As Big Medicine took over the responsibilty for health, the voices that spoke of obvious connections between lifestyle and disease were drowned out by the thundering stampede to junk food and irresponsible lifestyle. During this era of big fin cars, suburbia, ice cream with every meal and a pill for every ill, a purge of "unscientific" medicine began in the political halls and courts of North America. The almost hysterical self-righteousness of the medical profession and its political clout overwhelmed lifestyle-oriented physicians. Rights to practise were withdrawn in state after state, until naturopathy was confined mainly to a few Pacific Northwest states and a few Canadian provinces.

That the demise of alternate practioners in the U.S. has been high-handed is well-documented. The following is the initial decision by Administrative Law Judge, Ernest G. Barnes, Docket No. 9064, dated November 13, 1978:

" The Federal Court determined that the AMA has produced a formidable impediment to competition in the delivery of health care services by physicians in this country. That barrier has served to deprive consumers of the free flow of information about the availability of health care services, to deter the offering of innovative forms of health care and to stifle the rise of almost every type of health care delivery that could potentially pose a threat to the income of fee-for-services physicians in private practice. The costs to the public in terms of less expensive or even, perhaps, more improved forms of medical services are great."

In Canada similar events took place. In his book "Canadian Medicine: A Study in Limited Entry", Ronald Homowy summarizes:

" The following study's conclusions dispute the widely held belief that the various statutes and regulations raising the requirements for medical licensure were, in the first instance, enacted to protect the public from so-called incompetents. The historical data provide substantial evidence that the profession's motives in raising the standards of entry in medical practice and in instituting policies that prohibited advertising or any sort of price competition were almost purely ones of economic self-interest. . . . It is foolish to suppose that their occupation exalts them above using the means at their disposal to act in their own private interests."

Naturopathic training includes as much basic medical science as any health-care profession. Research is an important part of the naturopathic colleges. The quality of naturopathic education and a more open political environment have resulted in the passing of new laws in recent years in Washington, Oregon, Arizona and Alaska that have expanded the rights of naturopathic physicians to practise. Many other states are also considering expanding or relicensing this traditional approach to health care.

Speeding up your digestion by improving stomach function and following food combinations can result in virtual starvation for the intestinal competitors. The less food they digest, the less toxic stress on your system, the less free-radical irritation, the greater your body's inherent healing power. Homeostasis can swing the pendulum away from disease and back to health.

Using inhibitors of the bad intestinal flora, at the same time as speeding up your digestion, can often boost the improvement greatly.

The most important inhibitors of intestinal baddies are lactobacillus acidophilus. These friendly bacteria are the ones that turn milk into yogurt. The bacteria are most active if the yogurt is used when fresh, meaning within a day of making. It should also be used in proper combination.

Since the acidophilus only lives in the intestine for a few hours before it dies, we usually take it in capsules two or three times per day. Taking it after meals results in some of the bacteria being killed by the digestive juice, though some get through. It's a little more effective taking it about half an hour before meals.

We use capsules that also have lactobacillus bifidus with the acidophilus. This is the cousin of acidophilus and is the one that thrives best on mother's milk. It is the most common type of intestinal flora until about seven years of age, when the acidophilus predominates.

There are other species of lactobacillus bacteria used in making sourdough, which is more beneficial than bread that is only raised by yeast.

Some of the other things known to inhibit yeast are garlic, lemon, chlorophyll (found in greens) and oxygen. No doubt there are many more, especially in many of the herbs.

Free radicals and prostaglandins cannot be stored because they only exist for a fraction of a second. However, there is an actual physical storage of toxins that takes place, because in some people one of the first signs of increased vitality is feeling worse, as the body quickly puts its new-found energy into "housecleaning".

Withdrawal symptoms are well-known and are often seen when stimulants such as coffee, tobacco, chocolate or alcohol are removed. Besides the short-term headaches, disorientation, moodiness and fatigue during withdrawal from these drugs, there can be any number of symptoms as the body takes its surplus of digestive energy and tries to eliminate years of stored toxins.

Most of the toxins are stored in the large intestine area, apparently in the membranes. This may be because toxins produced in the intestine irritate the intestinal membrane. The membrane then makes mucous to protect itself. If the toxic irritation continues, then the mucous actually may form a coating over the membranes which can eventually thicken, trapping the toxins in it. As long as the toxins are held in this way they can't get absorbed and generate free radicals and bad prostaglandins, but they can't be eliminated from the body either.

This gradually-thickening mucous coating will reduce the absorption of toxins into the blood. Of course it will also decrease the absorption of nutrients.

As formation of intestinal toxins quickly decreases with speeding up of the digestion, the body may rapidly break up this mucous coating and release its stored toxins. If they are then absorbed into the blood they may cause symptoms to temporarily worsen.

It's not unusual to see strings of mucous in the stool, sometimes blood-tinged, for a short period of time, possibly because of the removal of this coating. To aid this removal of intestinal mucous there

are several things that can be used. One is psyllium hulls, which are
the seeds of the plantain plant. They are used in powdered form.
When water is added it swells into a jelly-like mass. This provides
bulk to help bowel movements without the scratchiness of bran. If a
large quantity of psyllium is taken at one time, it can form a ball
which can block the intestine for a few days, so the better way is to
take a small amount at the start, perhaps 1 tsp. two times a day before meals and slowly increase the quantity so that the intestine
gradually gets filled.

Clay is sometimes used in conjunction with psyllium. The most
common type used is called bentonite. It works as an astringent,
pulling the toxins out of the membrane into the intestine rather than
releasing them into the blood.

The result of detoxifying the intestine will be increased absorption
of nutrients, often very noticeable to a person as an improved sense
of well-being. The loss of this membrane coating will, however, also
make a person more sensitive, as dietary indiscretions that place
even small amounts of toxins in the large intestine will result in
greater absorption of them as well. So a person may experience insomnia after one cup of coffee at night, while before detoxification it
may have taken several cups for that to happen.

In some ways it makes this approach to health a one-way street.
Once you're into it there's no way out. As the organs start working

better most people usually feel much better quickly. Since now the organs tell the person when he or she is making mistakes rather than just staying passively in a state of shock, what a person can get away with is apparently reduced.

This is a bit of an illusion, as the person didn't really get away with anything before. It was just they didn't experience any immediate reaction to whatever they ate or drank, so they may have assumed it wasn't bad for them. In fact the body did have a bad reaction but didn't have the strength to indicate it. It's these many little accumulated suppressed reactions that eventually add up to "sudden" breakdowns such as heart attacks or cancer many years later.

If old toxins are stirred up faster than the elimination organs can handle them, a person can feel worse for a while. This used to be a major problem in my practise, but with a little experience I've managed to greatly reduce the incidences of healing crises.

Anyone who has a chronic disease has already overloaded the elimination organs. It doesn't take very much "stirring up" to overwhelm the already-overloaded organs, especially the lymph system.

Fortunately there is a pumping system to keep the lymph flowing. While the blood has the reliable heart to pump its rich cargo through the red sea of life, the lymph and veins are pumped by the contractions of the skeletal muscles of the body, through exercise. Exercise is important for proper waste elimination.

I must add that of all the professional and Olympic athletes I've seen, none of them tested as having the digestive and lymph systems working up to par either, so exercise is not a cure-all that can totally replace improving diet and digestion. Obviously the way to keep the lymph system clear is to minimize the metabolic debris that it has to handle, by having quick and efficient digestion.

There are some tricks that can be played on the lymph system as well. The tonsils are the part of the lymph system that are best known. They are commonly aggravated in children and can be tremendously swollen. The key to a lasting cure is of course attending to the digestive system, but short-term improvement can sometimes be gained with direct physical pressure on them.

The tonsils are normally soft, somewhat sponge-like. They get harder as they swell with toxic matter. If they are "squeezed", sometimes this toxic material will squirt right out of the tonsil. This is achieved by putting a finger down the side of the throat, so as to reduce gagging. Then when contact is made on the tonsil it is squeezed against the side of the throat. If good contact is made often quantities of foul toxins will be squeezed out, and sometimes dramatic improvements in overall health can occur. Since doing this is startling and causes gagging, I seldom do it myself but rather show patients how to do it and let them decide if it's worth it to them. One patient found she gagged less if she used the handle of a long spoon. This usually has to be repeated frequently until the dietary changes start to have an effect.

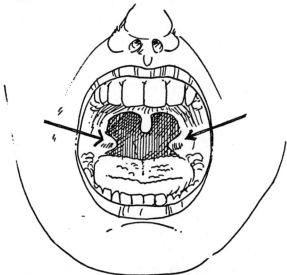

The glands of the neck are often swollen, and can be assisted in draining by massaging the neck in a downward direction. Since specific muscles pump specific parts of the lymph system, stimulation of a muscle will result in greater flow of lymph from its associated organ.

Testing indicates that the muscles most in need of stimulation are the tensor facia latae muscles found on the outside of the thighs. These muscles pump the lymph flow from the large intestine, which of course is where most of the toxins originate. Stimulation is done by vigorously rubbing the leg with a bristly shower brush, loofa or skin brush so that it is lightly irritated. Rubbing the inside of the thigh will also stimulate the small intestine lymph.

Rubbing the chest area will stimulate kidneys, liver, pancreas, stomach and gallbladder. Many of the muscles that pump these organs' lymph drainage are found between the ribs and are associated with breathing, so breath is not only important for its vital delivery of oxygen but also for helping to pump the drainage of toxins.

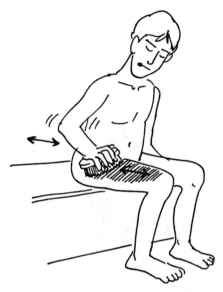

It only takes a few minutes every day while in the shower to give these areas a quick rub and thereby give the lymph system a little boost.

Lymphatic baths can be done several ways.

One way is to dissolve four pounds of Epsom salts in hot water.

Don't stay longer than fifteen minutes, and don't repeat for a week or so.

Also, you can add two pounds each of sea salt and baking soda to warm or hot water, and soak twenty to twenty-five minutes. For more information on baths see "Psychoimmunity and the Healing System", edited by Jason Serinus.

Another way is to draw a warm bath with approximately one cup of Chlorox bleach added. Soak for fifteen to thirty minutes and then follow with a normal shower. Keep head and hair out of the water.

The white blood cells are more active at slightly higher-than-normal body temperatures. The body creates fever as a way to enhance immune system function. The body temperature can be elevated for hours after vigorous excercise, during which period the white blood cell activity is accelerated.

The use of sweat lodges and saunas is universal among cultures in the temperate climates as a means of purification. In most long-term uses of heat, it is important to follow the hot with cold, as excess heat weakens the body while cold stimulates and tonifies.

The Finns are famous for their saunas and also for the high rate of heart attacks. One study showed there was a correlation between the two. Those who went right from the very hot to the very cold were the ones who had the most heart attacks. The sudden exposure to cold stimulates the heart to beat rapidly, but most of the blood still is in the arms and legs, and there isn't enough blood for the heart to function properly. Those who expose their arms and legs to cold first, to put the blood back into the chest before exposing it to cold, don't have such high rates of heart attack.

In the early stages of a cold, a hot bath before bed accompanied by extra covers can induce a fever which might burn up the cold over-night. It is also useful to take two grams of vitamin C about every hour until diarrhea is induced. The vitamin C works both as a buffer of toxins and as a mild laxative if enough is taken. The laxative effect is important, as you will find most acute illness preceded by a period of poor digestion. Bioflavenoids, especially rutin, work with vitamin C to inhibit viruses.

The white blood cells can be stimulated by a number of nutrients and herbs. This is too big a topic to cover in this book. Every naturopathic physician is trained to help boost the immune system as a way to aid a person to health.

Beets, both root and leaf, have been known to aid liver function. As the beet pigments discolor the stool, it's not unusual to have a patient think that there is blood in the stool when they start taking beets.

Dandelion root and leaf are also known to be good for the liver and skin, and are commonly used in liver formulas. Every company that makes nutritional products has its own formula for improving the liver. Methionine, inositol and choline are also common ingredients in these formulas, as they are important tools for the liver to detoxify efficiently.

The most important factor in keeping the stress off the gallbladder is to keep the ileocecal valve working properly. It is critical to not use any more scratchy fiber than the intestine can handle. Black radish tablets are sometimes useful to soothe the membranes of the intestine, so that the ileocecal valve becomes more resistent to abrasion. A long-term calcium deficiency often underlies a sensitive ilocecal valve. Silica extract (from horsetail herb), available from health food stores everywhere, may overcome this deficiency. Chlorophyll also sometimes aids the ileocecal valve to regain proper function as well as being soothing to intestinal membranes.

It is very important to keep the bowels regular during detoxification, even if laxatives or enemas need to be taken for a short time. If one is prone to constipation, it's good to stay away from constipating foods such as cheese and bananas, and to drink plenty of water. Start the day with soaked or stewed prunes, figs and raisins. Remember the stomach juices are the spark for proper functioning of the intestine.

Exercise is also important for proper bowel movements. Our bodies are designed to move. Movement puts pressure on the abdominal organs, including the intestine, and helps stimulate their proper function.

Walking is the cheapest and most available form of exercise. For the last hundred years mankind has put great effort into finding ways to avoid walking, but now we realize how important it is to exercise.

We have seen that exercise is important for stimulating the liver, and gallbladder and intestines, thus helping regular bowel movements, pumping the lymph and vein systems, and raising the body temperature, which in turn aids the immune system.

PATIENTS' LETTERS

I first visited your office, Dr. Matsen, in late December 1986, with symptoms of a virus infection diagnosed by a general practitioner ten years ago. I have had headaches, achy joints and muscles, very low energy and slowed thinking over this period. I had been given everything from aspirin to antibiotics with no improvement.

After your food sensitivity testing I started your diet and supplements. Since last March I had had no further attacks or symptoms!

> *Yours gratefully*
> *Mrs. Dorothy Atwell*

Dear Dr. Matsen

For approximately three months I was suffering considerably from severe pain in my right abdomen. During these three months my G.P. had prescribed pain killers; I had numerous blood tests, barium enema ex-rays, gynocological examinations, etc. to locate the cause of the pain—all without success.

On March 23, 1987, I had my first appointment with Dr. John Matsen. After a short discussion and examination he diagnosed the cause of the pain—the ileocecal valve. He prescribed hydrotherapy, a changed diet, and certain herb supplements. Within just three days the pain was gone, and within five weeks I was feeling terrific. The pain has not recurred and I don't need supplements.

> *A. Alderson*
> *North Vancouver*

CHAPTER 9

Three Stages to Health

Let's review what has been suggested so far for the three weeks of Phase I.

First, avoid food Groups I, II and III so the stomach can get back to work making those important digestive juices.

Second, do food combining, separating carbohydrates from proteins and fruit from grains and starches, to speed up the digestion so the intestinal critters don't make so many new toxins. Hypermetabolic people or those with severe metabolic imbalances, such as hypoglycemia, diabetes, epilepsy, narcolepsy, etc., should be under supervision and may be best off to skip Stage I and use the dietary guidelines of Stage III.

Third, take acidophilus and other critter inhibitors such as garlic, chlorophyll and lemon to slow down their digestion, to further reduce their toxin production.

Fourth, eat light foods in the morning as much as possible, so as to have a surplus of digestive juice, which will help clean out the old toxins.

Fifth, exercise regularly, do skin brushing and possibly liver/gallbladder and/or lymph supplementation, to help the elimination organs.

Now a sixth step can be added. In my practise we usually also do eight or nine hydrotherapy treatments, alternating hot and cold, and electronic stimulation. The effect is to gently "jump-start" the digestive organs and aid the elimination organs. Usually by the third or fourth hydrotherapy treatment a person begins to make surplus digestive juice which begins to clean out the old toxins.

How long should these activities be continued? It takes on average about three weeks for the major digestive organs to get "recharged". They are not fully recovered from years of abuse, but there is now "energy" going into them instead of draining out.

People with strong constitutions and high vitality may stir up the old toxins very quickly. If they also have weak elimination organs they may feel worse before feeling better, as they may not be able to eliminate the toxins as fast as they're being stirred up. People with weaker vitality may not experience this worsened feeling, as they usually will not stir things up very quickly. Of course their overall improvement will proceed at a slower rate.

Usually a person feels quite a bit better within three weeks, though it's not unusual to feel a little rough during the first week, due to a combination of withdrawal and detoxification. If cravings for sweets are are too strong, a mineral supplement high in magnesium, iodine and trace minerals will quickly dispel them. Bile salts can also reduce cravings for sweets in some people.

STAGE II

An interesting thing happens to food sensitivities after three weeks or so. On retesting, most people test strong to all Group IV foods and usually to Group III foods, as well as to all Group II foods except baking yeast. Group I usually still tests weak. The necessity for avoiding food combinations remains the same, except in people who are hypermetabolic.

Testing shows that they will do better mixing starches or grains with proteins.

During the three weeks we have succeeded in speeding up and improving the person's digestion and absorption, so that there are now more nutrients in the blood. At the same time digestion by the intestinal bad guys has been inhibited, so less toxins are now being deposited in the blood stream. Consequently, the cells get more nutrients, wastes are removed more quickly, and the body as a whole more readily regulates itself through homeostasis. If the healing capacity of the blood is now greater than the disease process, even chronic disease will quickly disappear.

Although the blood may be strong enough to heal chronic disease, the blood pictures show that it is seldom as good at this stage as it potentially could be. The key to understanding this is the fact that while most other foods now test as being okay, baking yeast will still test as a problem. Even though baking yeast is supposedly dead when baked in bread, it does test as weakening to the body when yeast within the body is a problem.

When after three weeks on the diet the baking yeast still tests weak while most other things are testing stronger, the yeast in the body is still there. However, the big party that the yeast has been having is over. The person is eating less of the foods that yeast thrives on and taking things that inhibit yeast and most importantly, digesting much more quickly. Since the bad flora now have less feeding time at your intestinal trough, they make fewer toxins. With fewer toxins to aggravate them, the function of the organs improves. The usual sequence in which the organs and glands become stronger is stomach, pancreas and parotid, small intestine, large intestine, liver, spleen and thymus, endocrine glands, and gallbladder. This is basically the reverse order in which they developed their problems. The sequence is affected by individual weaknesses, especially if organ damage exists.

This is usually the point where we add to yeast inhibitors the yeast killers. It's important that a person should feel fairly well at this point, or the yeast killer should be delayed. The reason is that as the yeast die off they are quite toxic and can foul up an already-overloaded elimination system, making the person feel considerably worse. By waiting until the digestion is improved and the elimination organs are strengthened before using yeast killer, there are two advantages.

1) You are stronger and the yeast is weaker, making it more certain to die off quickly. Thus you should only need to take yeast killer for a few weeks rather than the months to years that some people end up taking it.

2) Since your digestion is now working much more quickly, there isn't so much undigested food lying around for yeast to regrow on. By killing it off after improving digestion, you should only need to take the yeast killer once.

Compare this approach to dealing with mosquitoes. One can ignore them. This might be called the "Eastern" approach. Another way is to swat them one by one. This might be called the "Natural" approach. A third way is to engulf oneself and the area with poisonous chemicals. Call this the "Western" approach.

"EASTERN"   "NATURAL"   "WESTERN"

The fourth and most effective way may be to drain the swamp that the mosquitos breed in. The same is true of yeast. If you drain the "intestinal swamp" by first improving digestion, you will get rid of the yeast and you need never have a problem with it again, as there will now be no undigested food lying around for it to feast on.

There are a number of yeast killers available. The most consistently effective and readily available is caprylic acid. It is an eight-chain saturated fatty acid usually extracted from coconut fat or butter, and sold mainly through health food stores. There is no toxicity to caprylic acid as such, but because it is fatty it can be stressful to those who have major liver or gallbladder problems.

The effectiveness of caprylic acid is also its main drawback. The yeast often dies off very quickly and can cause dramatic temporary reactions in some people. A way to reduce the impact of these reactions is to start with three capsules with each meal for an adult for two days. If there is no reaction after two days, increase to four capsules twice a day for two days. If there is no reaction, increase to five, and so on until taking eight capsules twice a day. If there is a reaction at (say) five capsules twice a day, go back to four or less until feeling better, then slowly increase again.

I suggest using it twice a day because our program favours two meals a day. If a person has to have three full meals per day due to need for higher calorie intake because of heavier physical exertion or exposure to cold, or as an aid to stabilizing hypoglycemia, then he/she should take the caprylic acid three times per day with meals. Starting with two three times per day for two days, increase to three three times, until gradually working up to five three times per day. Again, if a bad reaction is experienced, reduce the dose immediately.

There are other yeast killers that aren't in a fatty base that can be used in liver/gallbladder problems or by children. Since these aren't readily available, you should consult your naturopath.

Yeast are seldom the only "critters" inhabiting the intestine. However, killing the yeast often will eliminate the toxic environment that these bad guys need to thrive in as well as decreasing the load on the immune system.

Some readily-available products that help inhibit or kill other parasites are pumpkin seeds for tapeworms, garlic for pinworms, and enzymes such as bromelain found in pineapple or papain found in papaya which help to digest a number of different organisms. If enzymes are taken with a meal they help to digest protein. If taken between meals they get into the bloodstream where they help do housecleaning including eating away at critters. Other things are

available through your naturopathic physician to help boost your
immune system.

STAGE III

If you've had a puppy with worms, you know the incredible boost
in vitality that can occur after they've been removed. When a person
is retested after taking yeast killers a similar thing is apparent. Virtually everything tests strong. All Group IV, Group III and Group II
foods test strong. Sometimes even some of the Group I non-foods
such as sugar test strong, but this usually only lasts for a few days.

Even the combinations change. After the yeast killers, fruit with
grains tests okay. Grains or starches with proteins test okay. However, protein tested with sweets, (even with many of the sweet
fruits) still tests as a problem. The sub-acid fruits are less of a problem. Sometimes an acid, such as cider vinegar or lemon used with
sweet and protein, will antidote the weakness.

How do we explain this? Mixing fruit with grains, or proteins
with grains, slows down digestion, but the yeast isn't waiting in the
intestine in large quantities now to jump in and make toxins. Mixing
the proteins and sweets, however, slows down digestion so much

that although the yeast isn't there to make toxins, "good" bacteria switch their white hats to black hats and start to make toxins.

A sub-acid or acid fruit may stimulate the stomach enough to overcome some of the stomach inhibiting effect of the sweet. It may be pushing one's luck to try these combinations. However, there seems to always be a limit to how long food can sit undigested in that dark, damp, warm, germ-infested tube we call the intestine. Before the increase of yeast-related problems brought about by antibiotics and refined carbohydrates such as white sugar and white flour, people could undoubtedly eat starches, grains and proteins together routinely without any adverse side-effects. Since sweets were rare in peasant cultures, they had little problem with mixing sweets and protein, and if they did have problems their elimination organs and immune systems could quickly deal with them.

Civilized diets inevitably offer more and more temptations to the palate. Affections of children are bought with sweets, and dessert with meals becomes routine as income increases. As the elimination organs and immune system become fouled up, medication becomes necessary to "save" the helpless person. The downward spiral in health has begun.

After regaining efficient digestion and THEN killing off the competing intestinal critters, the quality of a person's blood usually improves dramatically, sometimes to perfection. The blood has reached its ideal state: rich with all the necessary nutrients and low in irritating toxins. The cells receive all the raw materials they need and their wastes are readily removed. Homeostasis is in control, and when you reach this state you can virtually feel your blood "purr" through your body.

What happens from this point depends mainly on the vitality of the person. If one has high vitality and few accumulated toxins it isn't too necessary to pay heed to food combinations other than to avoid mixing sweets and proteins. Eating lightly in the morning when possible will usually be enough to continue a gradual detoxification. Of course, remaining on the stricter regime can only add to already bountiful health.

A person with average vitality and a fair amount of toxins accumulated over years of digestive malfunction, but no real chronic disease, should continue to eat lightly in the morning to continue removing the old metabolic debris. Such a person should continue to separate the starches and grains from the proteins. A little starch or grain with protein once in a while usually isn't a problem. For example, barley in chicken soup is no problem. Many of the ethnic ways of eating, using small amounts of protein with starch or grain, are no problem occasionally.

However, a person with weak vitality, large amounts of accumulated toxicity and/or chronic disease will need to remain on the stricter regime much longer. Stage I or II should be maintained as long as necessary so the surplus digestive energy can go out into the bloodstream. It takes time to chip away those years of accumulated fat and metabolic debris. Ideally, such a person should be under the supervision of a naturopath. A sedentary person usually feels best on Stages I and II. Homeopathic remedies can sometimes rebuild depleted vitality. There are also supplements to aid the removal of old accumulated toxins. Every naturopath is experienced in detoxification, as this has been the underlying theme of Naturopathy for hundreds of years. Professional guidance can save a lot of time and money, and prevent complications when intensive detoxification is necessary.

No practitioner or philosophy can help every patient in every circumstance. I have sent hundreds of patients to medical doctors, chiropractors, physiotherapists, massage therapists, psychologists, etc., because they could give better care for a particular problem than I could.

The most important thing that you should have gained from this program is sensitivity. You should now know when you have eaten something wrong, as your once-spasmed and somewhat muted stomach should now be talking back in full voice. Sometimes the message won't come right after eating something. Maybe the message will be in the form of cloudy thinking or moodiness a day or two after, but if you're paying attention you will see now that your digestion is affecting every little nuance of your life. At this point diet books, including this one, will have lost much of their value. Now, instead of being told what you should and shouldn't eat, you can get that information directly from the best teacher you could have, your own body.

Sometimes people stray farther than they should, and regain their old problems or even gain new ones as the digestive strength begins to wane. Sometimes they panic and forget what to do to reverse the problem. Simply start again at the beginning of this program or go to see your naturopath.

PATIENT'S LETTER

I first went to see Dr. Matsen in 1984 for psoriasis as I was dissatisfied with the dermatologist's creams, ointments and impersonal care which seemed to have little or no effect. After about four months of my personalized diet and specific supplements from Dr. Matsen the symptoms disappeared, although the psoriasis reoccurs at times if I go too far off the diet.

In January, 1987, I experienced abdominal pain and frequent blood and mucous in diarrhea. When this continued for a couple of weeks I went to a medical doctor who referred me to a gastro-intestinal (G.I.) specialist. He gave me an internal examination and blood tests and x-rays including a colonoscopy. For this ordeal I was an outpatient at St. Paul's Hospital where after several enemas and an injection of barium, a length of hose with a lighting device and microscope was inserted. The doctor, assistant and I could watch a monitor or actually look into the tube and see the colon. I was really impressed with this technology but the pain was excruciating. After this and x-ray results the diagnosis was ulcerative colitis.

The G.I. specialist had prescribed tablets that would control the symptoms, although the side effects included nausea, headaches and possible financial hardship (they cost sixty dollars a month). I asked if a change in diet or lifestyle would help. His response was "Oh, no, it's not uncommon for a person your age (I'm thirty-four) to have colitis, but it is treatable. This is very serious and you'll probably take medication the rest of your life . . . but there's nothing else you can do."

I was not satisfied with this and definitely not interested in taking any prescription for the rest of my life. So I went to see Dr. Matsen again. When I told him the diagnosis, his warm and optimistic response was "We'll have you fixed up in a couple of weeks!" What a relief. He humourously explained what was going on in my digestive system and why my white blood cells were attacking my intestine. With a combination of hydrotherapy, a return to my original diet that I had wandered from, a few supplements and my personal committment to get well, I am now relieved of my symptoms and apparently cured of colitis, and in only five weeks.

Jan Stephenson
Vancouver, B.C.

PART III

MENU PLANS AND RECIPES

CHAPTER 10

Introduction

It is impossible to tell people exactly what to eat and when to eat it. Different people have different metabolisms, affected by weather, type of work, stress and organ function, never mind a wide variety of tastes. People with metabolic imbalances such as hypoglycemia, diabetes, epilepsy, narcolepsy, or are overly metabolic, that is they burn up calories rapidly and have trouble gaining weight, should be under supervision and possible need to start at Stage III.

The Menu Plans are only very general guidelines and are not to be taken dogmatically. The closer you can follow them the better but don't worry if you can't.

In theory a person should be able to go only on water for three days or so with little fluctuation in their energy. However, few people these days have organs that function that well. Detoxifying them will eventually greatly improve their function but at the beginning you may only be able to eat light in the morning for a short period of time. How long that is is entirely up to you. Get a little hungry in the morning before you actually eat a meal but don't leave it so long that you actually get weak and lightheaded. If it's only a few minutes that's okay, that's a few minutes that the body was able to detoxify and the next day you might be able to go a few minutes longer. If you're doing heavy physical labour or sports, especially in cold weather, you might need a large breakfast. Try and make up for it by going lighter on your days off.

Many of the recipes take time and not everyone takes time to prepare their own food. If you use restaurants try to avoid the deep fry places as much as you can. Many of the better restaurants menus are a la carte so food combining needn't be a problem. Many restaurants will substitute to your direction and not use MSG if you ask. If it's necessary to break the combinations, things like soup, even if not combined properly, are often easy to digest. Try to avoid heavy sauces. Most vegetarian restaurants are quite careful as to their ingredients.

The more relaxed you are, the better your digestion works. The more you chew the less strain on the pancreas. Drinking while eating interferes with production of digestive juice. Drinking of most liquids after eating dilutes the digestive juice thus slowing digestion. Water however can get past the food and into the intestine without interfering with digeston. Overeating will bog down the digestive system for hours and certainly prevent any surplus digestive juice being available for detoxifying. Undereating can result in deficiencies of calories, proteins, vitamins, minerals, essential fatty acids, fiber and force the body to cannibalize itself to provide fuel. This is the point where fasting becomes starvation and is seen often because of the emphasis that fashion has placed on leanness rather than health.

In practise it's not unusual to have a person reverse a chronic disease only to return at a future date with the same or similar symptoms. Only rarely has the stomach returned to its earlier "shocked" state even if they have wandered widely from an ideal diet. Occasionally the yeast has returned, usually a result of eating excess sweets. Sweet fruit such as bananas used liberally, especially in winter, can bring yeast back. However, by far the most common problem that people return with is malfuncton of the ileocecal valve and resultant gallbladder problems due to excessive use of fresh fruits and raw vegetables, coarse grains and sometimes spices. This is especially seen in the fall and winter. The reason is that fresh fruits and raw vegetables are hot-season foods that cool the body, especially the kidney meridian. Since the ileocecal valve is on the kidney meridian it gets more sensitive as the weather cools if summer foods are maintained. Thus as fruits pass out of season they should be used less, or, if at all, should be used warm. Therefore, hot applesauce would be better than fresh apples in winter. The hot lemon drink is excellent in cold weather. As salad season ends, vegetables should be cooked more: steamed, stir-fried or in soups and stews. Hot cereals such as oatmeal are great in cold weather.

The menu plans are not designed with a particular season in mind so you will have to adapt them to suit your own needs.

Good eating and great digestion!

STAGE I DIET

7 Days of Sample Menus

DAY 1 — Monday
a.m. Citrus —Lemon Drink
(One half hour to 1 hour before other fruits)

a.m. "Breakfast"
apples

a.m. Snack "Pick-me-up"
(Optional 2 hrs. after fruit.)
vegetable juice (¾ cup carrot juice mixed with ¼ cup beet juice)

Lunch/Dinner
(Anytime from 10:00 a.m. —if snack is omitted—to 3:00 p.m. as desired) Serve about 2 hrs. after snack or 4 hrs. after fruit.)
1. *Spinach Salad* with a vegetable dressing
2. *Lentil Soup*
3. *Sourdough Rye Bread, Flatbreads* or rice or rye crackers

Supper
(any time from 5:00 p.m. to 9:00 p.m. —should be finished at least 2 hrs. before bedtime)
1. Sliced or chopped vegetables with almond or cashew nut butter (as a dip or spread)—try carrot sticks, cucumber sticks or rounds, green or red bell pepper strips, broccoli trees and/or cauliflower flowerets
2. *Broiled Salmon Steaks or Fillets*
3. Steamed Greens—kale, chard, mustard, beet greens or other greens

* Italicized titles of recipes are recipes found within this book.

DAY 2 — Tuesday
a.m. Citrus—Lemon Drink
(One half hour to 1 hour before other fruits)

a.m. "Breakfast"
plums (in season) or pears

a.m. Snack "Pick-me-up"
(Optional 2 hrs. after fruit.)
Carrot Soup

Lunch/Dinner
1. Avocado half stuffed with sunflower seeds
2. *Brown Rice* with *Curried Red Lentils*
3. *Chick Pea or Lentil Chipatis*

Supper
1. Any leafy green salad with dressing
2. *Herb Scrambled Eggs*
3. Baked or steamed broccoli, zucchini or kohlrabi

DAY 3 — Wednesday
a.m. Citrus—Lemon Drink
(One half hour to 1 hour before other fruits)

a.m. "Breakfast"
grapes

a.m. Snack "Pick-me-up"
(Optional 2 hrs. after fruit)
Vegetable Soup

Lunch/Dinner
1. *Rice Salad* with dressing—try *Herb & Oil* or a vegetable dressing
2. *Chick Pea-Vegetable Spread* spread on:
3. Rye or rice crackers or *Flatbreads*

Supper
1. *Wild Salad* with fresh lemon juice OR *Romaine Salad*

2. *Garlic (or Herb Baked) Chicken*
3. Sauteed or steamed carrots, cauliflower and green beans or peas medley

DAY 4 — Thursday
a.m. Citus—fresh grapefruit halves
(One half hour to 1 hour before other fruits)

a.m. "Breakfast"
unusual fruit—Japanese pears or Japanese pear-apples (if un-available—use regular pears)

a.m. Snack "Pick-me-up"
(Optional 2 hrs. after fruit
Vegetable Broth

Lunch/Dinner
1. Celery chunks and/or green pepper quarters and/or cucumber rounds spread or stuffed with:
2. *Falafel Spread*
3. *Flatbreads*, rice or rye crackers

Supper
1. *Oriental Salad* with *Lemon-Oil Dressing*
2. *Egg Foo Yong*
3. *Arrowroot Sauce* (Delicious gravy to top Egg Foo Yong with!)

DAY 5 — Friday
a.m. Citus—Lemon Drink
(One half hour to 1 hour before other fruits)

a.m. "Breakfast"
melon—cantaloupe, honeydew or watermelon

a.m. Snack "Pick-me-up"
(Optional 2 hrs. after fruit
Green Drink

Lunch/Dinner
1. Carrot and celery sticks
2. *Kidney Bean Stew*

Supper
1. Carrot juice cocktail with added broccoli or parsley juice
2. *Beet Treat*
3. *Stir-Fry Vegetables* with one of the following: pre-cooked chunks of beef, chicken or salmon OR raw baby shrimp or tofu chunks

DAY 6 — Saturday
a.m. Citrus—fresh grapefruit halves
(One half hour to 1 hour before other fruits)

a.m. "Breakfast"
berries or cherries (in season) or grapes

a.m. Snack "Pick-me-up"
Miso Soup

Lunch/Dinner
1. *Bean Tacos* on corn tortillas topped with raw, chopped green or red bell peppers, lettuce, spinach or sprouts, zucchini chunks, sliced black olives and diced red or green onions or chives
2. *Guacamole* (to top tacos with)

Supper
1. *Super Sprout Salad*
2. *Broiled or Baked Trout, Sole, Cod* or other fish
3. *Steamed Artichoke* with melted butter

DAY 7 — Sunday
a.m. Citrus—fresh grapefruit halves
(One half hour to 1 hour before other fruits)

a.m. "Breakfast"
peaches or apricots

a.m. Snack "Pick-me-up"
(Optional 2 hrs. after fruit
vegetable juice (½ carrot, ½ celery and 2–3 sprigs parsley)

Lunch/Dinner
1. *Stuffed Green Peppers*
2. *Vegetarian Gravy* (over peppers)
3. *Baked Turnips* or steamed parsnips

Supper
1. *Zucchini Salad*
2. *Shisk Kebabs* with shrimp, chicken, turkey or tofu pieces
3. Optional: leftover soup from the week

ALTERNATE VEGETARIAN SUPPER SUGGESTION

1. *Baked Butternut Squash* with cinnamon
2. *Tofu Spread* with:
3. Rye crackers, corn chips or *Flatbreads*
4. *Split Pea Soup*

EXTRA SNACK SUGGESTIONS

1. Sesame tahini *or* almond *or* cashew nut butter stuffed in celery
2. Sesame tahini on rice cakes or crackers or rye crackers
3. *Tofu Spread* on cucumber rounds
4. *Spinach-Tofu Spread* with cut vegetables
5. Raw almonds or cashews (chewed well)
6. Sunflower seeds and/or sprouts
7. *Pumpkin, Carrot or Zucchini Muffins*
8. *Guacamole* and corn chips
9. *Eggsalad* with vegetable sticks or stuffed in celery
10. Popcorn with butter and sea salt
11. *Falafel or Chick Pea-Vegetable Spread* with vegetables

12. Half an avocado stuffed with *Tofu Spread*
13. Half an avocado stuffed with sunflower seeds *or* almonds or cashews
14. Unsweetened *Applesauce* (homemade)
15. *Soy Cashew Nuts*
16. Leftover soups

STAGE II DIET

7 Days of Sample Menus

DAY 1 — Monday

a.m. "Breakfast"
pears

a.m. Snack "Pick-me-up"
(Optional 2 hrs. after fruit.)
Vegetable Soup
OR
Between 8 & 11 a.m. (Optional 2 hrs. after fruit and 2 hrs. or more before lunch)
Breakfast Cereal or Yogurt
OR
Millet Cereal with a bit of honey, maple syrup or molasses cooked into it *or* served with sea salt and butter

Lunch/Dinner
1. *Rice* or *Romaine Salad*
2. *Cold Bean Balls or Pate*
3. *Sourdough Rye* or wheat bread or crackers (no yeast)

Supper
1. *Spinach Salad* (Optional: add tomatoes and/or possibly a yogurt dressing)
2. Turkey with:
3. *Arrowroot Sauce* (Delicious Gravy)—some of the turkey drippings can be used instead of water in the sauce
4. Sauteed Broccoli with sliced almonds (use oil and tamari soy sauce for sauteing)

DAY 2 — Tuesday

a.m. "Breakfast"
bananas

a.m. Snack "Pick-me-up"
(Optional 2 hrs. after fruit)
Vegetable Broth
OR
Breakfast Cereal or Yogurt
OR
Toast or *Muffins* with butter

Lunch/Dinner
1. Avocado half stuffed with sunflower seeds
2. *Kidney Bean Stew*

Supper
1. *Wild Salad* or other leafy green salad with dressing
2. *Broscht* (Optional: served with buttermilk cheese or yogurt)
3. *Easy Tuna or Salmon Bake*

DAY 3 — Wednesday

a.m. "Breakfast"
melon *or* grapes

a.m. Snack "Pick-me-up"
(Optional 2 hrs. after fruit)
Carrot Soup
OR
Breakfast Cereal or Yogurt
OR
Sweet Rice Cereal with a bit of honey,maple syrup or molasses
cooked into it *or* served with sea salt and butter

Lunch/Dinner
1. Raw vegetables stuffed in
2. *Falafel Sandwiches* served in

3. *Sourdough Rye Bread* or *Flatbreads*

Supper
1. *Super Sprout Salad* (Optional: add tomatoes and/or possibly a yogurt dressing)
2. *Spanish Omelet*

DAY 4 — Thursday

a.m. "Breakfast"
apricots or peaches

a.m. Snack "Pick-me-up"
(Optional 2 hrs. after fruit)
vegetable juice (¾ cup carrot juice with ¼ cup beet juice)
OR
Breakfast Cereal or Yogurt
OR
Wheat Berry Cereal (plain—bit of sea salt optional)

Lunch/Dinner
1. *Beet Treat* with avocado slices
2. *Sweet and Sour Lentils*
3. Crackers, *Flatbreads* or *Sourdough Rye* or Wheat

Supper
1. *Zucchini Salad* (tomatoes may be added)
2. *Turkey Soup*
3. Steamed or baked cauliflower, carrots, green beans or peas medley

DAY 5 — Friday

a.m. "Breakfast"
Lemon Drink

a.m. Snack "Pick-me-up"
(Optional 2 hrs. after fruit)

Miso Soup
OR
Breakfast Cereal or Yogurt
OR
Leftover cereal from the week

Lunch/Dinner
1. Celery and carrot sticks
2. *Split Pea Soup*
2. Corn chips, bread or crackers

Supper
1. Avocado half stuffed with almonds and topped with yogurt
2. Beef Steak or *Salmon Steaks*
3. *Ratatouille*

DAY 6 — Saturday

a.m. "Breakfast"
apples

a.m. Snack "Pick-me-up"
(Optional 2 hrs. after fruit)
Green Drink
OR
Breakfast Cereal or Yogurt
OR
Yogurt with fresh pineapple and/or shredded coconut
OR
Yogurt with chopped papaya or kiwi

Lunch/Dinner
1. *Oriental Salad*
2. *Broiled Tofu Burger* served on:
3. Bread or bun (yeast-free) or with crackers *or* serve with corn on the cob
4. Serve burger with spinach or sprouts and *Super Sandwich Topping*

Supper
1. *Beet Treat Salad* (Optional: with buttermilk cheese)
2. *Shrimp Creole* served over:
3. Steamed cauliflower (broken into flowerets and sliced)

DAY 7 — Sunday

a.m. "Breakfast"
fresh grapefruit halves

a.m. Snack "Pick-me-up"
(Optional 2 hrs. after fruit)
Vegetable Soup or vegetable juice (for juice try: ½ cup carrot, ½ cup celery or broccoli and 2–3 sprigs parsley)
OR
Breakfast Cereal or Yogurt
OR
Cornmeal Cereal with sweetening, cinnamon, sea salt and butter

Lunch/Dinner
1. Green pepper slices or cucumber or celery sticks
2. *Baked Beans*
3. *Sourdough bread* or *Flatbreads* or corn chips or crackers
4. *Baked Butternut or Acorn Squash* with cinnamon

Supper
1. *Greek Salad* (Optionals: use tomatoes instead of red bell peppers, and/or add 2–4 Tbsp. feta cheese
2. Roast lamb or beef or chicken
3. Cooked Greens (steamed or sauteed) kale, chard, mustard, beet greens or other greens
4. *Baked Turnips* or steamed turnips

ALTERNATE VEGETARIAN SUPPER SUGGESTIONS

Choose a Lunch or Supper from *Stage I* or repeat a Lunch from *Stage II*.

EXTRA SNACK SUGGESTIONS

1. Any snack from *Stage I*
2. Plain yogurt
3. Yogurt with fresh pineapple and/or shredded coconut
4. Yogurt with cut papaya or kiwi
5. Yogurt with grated cucumber and its juice with paprika or cumin sprinkled on (a bit of lemon juice may be added too)
6. *Buttermilk Cheese*
7. *Spinach-Tofu Spread* with crackers or bread
8. *Tofu Spread* with crackers or bread
9. *Banana or Apple Raisin Bread or Muffins*
10. Yogurt with chopped almonds or cashews

STAGE III DIET

7 Days of Sample Menus

DAY 1 — Monday

a.m. "Breakfast"
plums or grapes

Breakfast
(Optional 1–2 hrs. after fruit)
(Morning soups and cereals may be substituted here as needed or
desired)
1. Granola with:
2. Milk or apple juice
OR
1. French toast with:
2. Syrup and/or cooked fruit

Lunch/Dinner
1. Tomatoes, avocado halves or a green bell pepper stuffed with:
2. *Eggsalad* or *Tofu Spread*
3. Pecans or filberts or brazil nuts

Supper
1. *Spinach Salad* (tomatoes may be added)
2. *Spaghetti* or *Lasagna Rice* with tomato sauce and parmesan
cheese (browned ground beef may be added to the sauce if desired)
3. Steamed or baked broccoli or zucchini with butter OR *Broccoli or
Zucchini Soup*

DAY 2 — Tuesday

a.m. "Breakfast"
peaches or apricots

Breakfast
(Optional 1–2 hrs. after fruit)
1. *Millet* or *Sweet Rice Cereal* with
2. Sweetenings *or* butter and sea salt *Dates, apricots or other dried fruit may be cooked into the cereal for sweetening if desired

Lunch/Dinner
1. *Spinach Salad* (tomatoes may be added, use any dressing)
2. *Vegetable Quiche*

Supper
1. Alfalfa sprouts with a creamy dressing
2. *Spiced Vegetables and Polenta* (4–6 oz. baby shrimp, shredded crab or cubed tofu may be added)

DAY 3 — Wednesday

a.m. "Breakfast"
Lemon Drink

Breakfast
(Optional 1–2 hrs. after fruit)
1. Milk or yogurt
2. 2–3 Eggs—fried, poached or other
3. Toast and jam (or Muffin)

Lunch/Dinner
1. *Romaine* or *Wild Salad*
2. *Lentil Tomato Soup* OR *Sweet and Sour Lentils*
3. Whole wheat pita, whole wheat, rye, eight grain or other bread (yeasted o.k.)

Supper
1. Raw and cooked vegetables (see *Gado-Gado recipe*) and
2. Chopped hard-boiled eggs with:
3. *Gado-Gado Peanut Sauce*

DAY 4 — Thursday

a.m. "Breakfast"
Lemon Drink

Breakfast
(Optional 1–2 hrs. after fruit)
1. Yogurt and fruit
2. Muffins

Lunch/Dinner
1. *Oriental Salad* (2 tsp. honey and 2 tsp. rice vinegar may be added to the marinade) OR *Super Sprout Salad* (tomatoes optional)
2. *Cashew Patties with Mushroom Gravy*

Supper
1. Any green leafy salad (no tomatoes)
2. *Confetti Rice* (Optional: added small chunks of cold ham, chicken, shrimp or marinated tofu)
3 *Arrowroot Sauce* (Delicious gravy to top Egg Foo Yong with!)

DAY 5 — Friday

a.m. "Breakfast"
apples

Breakfast
(Optional 1–2 hrs. after fruit)
1. Milk or yogurt (optional)
2. *Oatmeal* with:
3. Cut fruit or sweetenings and cinnamon and a bit of sea salt

Lunch/Dinner
1.2.3. *Bean Tacos* with everything! (May include tomatoes and be topped with sour cream and salsa or picante sauce.)

Supper
1. *Fish in Cream Sauce* or *Clam Chowder*
2. *Stir-Fry Vegetables* with almonds or cashews (no meat or tofu)

DAY 6 — Saturday

a.m. "Breakfast"
melon

Breakfast
(Optional 1–2 hrs. after fruit)
Vegetable Soup OR Choose any breakfast

Lunch/Dinner
1. *Zucchini Salad* (tomatoes may be added)
2. *Lentil Burgers*
3. Whole wheat buns or bread on the side (yeasted o.k.)

Supper
1. *Baked Butternut or Acorn Squash* with cinnamon
2. Roast ham, beef, lamb, chicken or turkey
3. *Steamed Artichokes* with butter or a cream sauce

DAY 7 — Sunday

a.m. "Breakfast"
Oranges

Breakfast
(Optional 1–2 hrs. after fruit)
1. Milk or yogurt (optional)
2. Scrambled eggs or omelet

3. *Pancakes* (*Amazing Amaranth* or other) served with:

4. Cooked fruit toppings or applesauce

Lunch/Dinner

1. Optional: any green leafy salad

2. *Pita Pizzas*

Supper

1. *Spinach* or *Romaine Salad* (tomatoes may be used)

2. *Pecan-Cheese Loaf* with *Mushroom Gravy*

3. Cooked (steamed, baked or sauteed) broccoli, zucchini or kohlrabi

4. Optional: corn on the cob

IMPORTANT FOOD TIPS

1. ¾ tsp. sea salt equals 1 tsp. regular table salt. (Regular table salt contains sugar!)
2. When doubling a recipe only use 1½ times the amount of salt. When tripling a recipe—double the salt.
3. When oil is used in recipes, try a light-coloured, natural, cold-pressed variety. As with all natural oil products, (including mayonnaise and salad dressings) refrigerate after opening. This is a must for safety and freshness!
4. Kelp (sea kelp) is an important food supplement. It contains iodine and other minerals and sea salt contains no iodine so kelp and sea salt are almost always used together. Kelp also adds flavour and gives body and depth to recipes. Enjoy it often for its many benefits.
5. All nuts and seeds should be chewed very well for proper digestion. Chew them to powder to mix lots of saliva with them and speed digestion.
6. All types of juices should be sipped very slowly and even swished in the mouth before swallowing to aid digestion and make all the nutrients they contain more easily and completely assimilated. Never gulp juices, savour them.
7. Never under or overcook foods. This may impair flavours and digestion. Don't eat foods reheated more than once as they have lost most of their nutrients but retained their calories!

HOW TO COOK BEANS PROPERLY FOR GOOD DIGESTION
(And No Gas!)

1. Measure the amount of beans (peas/legumes) required and sort through them and remove any misshapen, discoloured or dam-

aged beans. Also remove any dirt balls, gravel, or other foreign objects and discard them.

2. Soak 1 cup of dry beans in 3 to 4 cups of cool or room temperature water and let the beans soak 8 hours or more uncovered. (12 hours for chick peas (garbonzos) and 24 hours for soybeans) Avoid using soybeans as they usually require a pressure cooker.
3. Throw away the water the beans soaked in. (Very Important!)
4. Rinse the beans several times with fresh water.
5. Put the beans in a large pot so that beans fill only ¼ of the pot and add fresh water until the beans are covered by 1 inch or so of water.
6. Bring the beans and water, uncovered, to a boil on high heat.
7. When the beans are boiling, a white foam or froth will generally form on top. Scoop this off and discard it. This is part of what contributes to gas.
8. Add extra water if needed so the beans are still at least 1 inch under water and turn the heat down to very low. Just low enough so the beans are barely bubbling. They cook best at this temperature.
9. Add 1 tsp. ground fennel or preferably 1 tsp. savory to the beans, this also improves their digestibility. (Optional)
10. Cook for 1¼ hours or more until the beans are very tender and a bean can easily be mashed with the tongue on the roof of the mouth.
11. Always chew beans slowly, never eat them fast or when under excessive stress or tiredness.
12. Have some raw foods first in a meal before eating the beans to aid in their digestion.

WHOLE GRAINS

Whole grains are delicious, nutritious and more digestible than refined grains when properly prepared. They are also less likely to aggravate those with allergies, low blood sugar, diabetes, and candida or other health problems. They contain natural fiber and are lower in calories than many refined food products.

The whole grains are divided into two categories: cereal grains; and the main dish grains.

Special Tips About Grains

1. Grains are generally cooked in two cups of water or more per one cup of grain.
2. Cook grains until they are no longer crunchy, but not soggy or mushy.
3. Very few grains need to be soaked before cooking. These include: wild rice (sometimes), whole oats, and rye and wheat kernels (berries).
4. Raw rolled, flaked, or crushed grains must be soaked before eating. Toasted grains may be eaten as they are or with milk substitutes or fruit juices (apple, pear, and peach are excellent for this).
5. Before cooking, check grains for dirt balls, gravel, husks, and other foreign particles by spreading them out thinly and fingering through them.
6. Rice is usually the only grain that needs prewashing, but you may wash any grain if you feel it needs it.
7. It makes little difference if you start cooking a grain in cool or warm water. The exception is ground cereals. These get lumpy when put in warm water unless mixed in carefully with a wire wisk.
8. To prevent grains from boiling over and to distribute heat evenly, water and grains together should never cover more than three-fourths of the cooking pot.
9. Do not add salt or oil to whole grains until the last 10 to 15 minutes of cooking, to make digestion easier.
10. Any grain in *whole* form (does not include rolled or broken whole grains) will never burn during its *first* cooking process as long as the water does not run out and the grain does not become overcooked to the point that it falls apart. (It usually takes 1¼ hours or more for grains to fall apart and burn.) Also they must be cooked on low heat.
11. Never stir whole grains while cooking or they will stick and burn.
12. When reheating whole grains (second cooking), add a little extra water—about ¼ to ½ cup per cup of grain—cook the grain, covered, on a very low heat until warmed. Brown rice can be reheated by steaming in a vegetable steamer.
13. One cup of dry whole grain or cereal makes about four servings.

14. The main-dish grains can almost always be substituted one for the other in different recipes, except wild rice. Grains are similar, but may have slight taste differences.
15. Wheat, rye, barley and oats contain gluten.
16. Cereals may be served with milk on milk substitutes or juices in *Stage III* only.

PREPARATION OF CEREAL GRAINS
See Tip #16

Raw Cereals

Soaked Oats—ORGANIC ROLLED OATS—These are smaller and rounder than regular, natural rolled oats and must be soaked for several hours or overnight before eating, unless they are 'crushed' or chopped after rolling, then they cook as easily as the natural. Use 1 to 1½ cups water per 1 cup of oats. These are usually found only in health food stores and are almost always labelled *organic*. After soaking the oats, drain off excess water (if any) and serve with sweetening, milk substitute and/or fruit.

NATURAL ROLLED OATS—(Regular or Old-Fashioned)—Soak 1 cup oats in 1 cup of very warm water for 10 to 15 minutes. Add flavourings and/or cut fruit and serve.

Rolled Rice or Barley—Use instead of oats in recipes, if available.

Flaked Whole-Grain Cereals—Flaked oats, rye, (wheat), rice, barley and millet may be purchased, but are not always available. Prepare and serve them like soaked organic rolled oats or toast them in the oven like granola. Serve with milk substitute and flavourings.

Puffed Whole-Grain Cereals—These cereals include puffed oats, corn, rice, millet, (wheat), and others. They are usually unsweetened. Serve them as they are with milk substitute and sweetening as desired.

Muesli and Other Raw Cereals—These cereals are usually made with rolled, cracked, or flaked whole grains and ground or chopped nuts and seeds and sometimes shredded coconut, raisins, or other dried fruits. If the cereal is organic or contains very tough, fibrous grains, prepare it the same way as Soaked Organic Oats. If the cereal is just natural and less fibrous, prepare the same way as Soaked Natural Oats.

Granola and Other Toasted Grain Cereals—Made with toasted rolled oats, nuts and seeds, dried fruit, and sweetening, etc. Serve with milk substitute or eat right out of the package. Chew well.

Cooked Cereals

Cooked Oatmeal—ORGANIC OATMEAL—Use 1½ to 2 cups water per one cup organic rolled oats. Bring the water to a boil, then turn down heat and add oats. Stir oats constantly and cook for ten minutes or until oats are easy to chew. Then turn off heat and cover otameal and let it sit 10 to 15 minutes before serving. Add flavouring or fruit.

NATURAL OATMEAL AND CHOPPED, ROLLED ORGANIC OATMEAL—(Regular or Old-Fashioned)—Use 1¼ to 1¾ cups water per 1 cup natural rolled oats. Bring water to a boil and add oats. Stir for 1 minute, cover, remove from heat and let sit for 10 to 15 minutes before serving. Add flavourings.

Cornmeal—Use about 2 to 2½ cups water per 1 cup meal. The coarser the meal, the more water is needed and the longer the cooking time. Start water and meal cooking together in lukewarm water and stir together on a medium heat. Use a wire wisk to make sure the meal and water are well mixed together to avoid lumpy cereal. After the first minute or two, the cereal must be stirred constantly for 10 minutes or more until it is no longer grainy. Add extra water if needed. It should always have a sweetener like honey added to it. Raisins, dates, or coconut and cinnamon cooked into the cereal are also very delicious. Salt is optional. Store cornmeal used for cereal in a cool place, or in the freezer, but never refrigerate it or it will have a damp, musty flavour.

Millet (Cereal)—Use about 3 to 4 cups of water per 1 cup millet. More water is used for the cereal than for the main-dish millet. Bring water and millet to a boil. Dates can be added now if desired—delicious! Use about ¼ to ½ cup dates per 1 cup millet. Then turn down heat to a low bubble, keep pot covered, and cook about 50 to 60 minutes until the millet breaks down and is very soft and mushlike. Before serving, stir the cereal to mix in the dates.

Serve with milk substitute or juice and oil and also honey, if no dates are added. Add salt if desired.

Sweet Rice—Cook and serve like millet cereal above, except use 2 to 3 cups per 1 cup rice and cook it for about 50 to 60 minutes until tender.

Whole Oats—Cook the same as the main dish. Serve plain with salt or with oil and honey, or maple syrup added.

PREPARATION OF MAIN-DISH GRAINS

Short- and Long-Grain Brown Rice—Put rice in a pot and fill it with water. Rub the rice together with hands and swish it around to remove excess starches, dirt, and stray rice husks. Toss out all the water. If water was very cloudy during the first washing, repeat the process once or twice until the water remains relatively clear. Then put 2 to 2¼ cups water per 1 cup rice in the pot on medium heat and bring it to a boil. Then turn down to a low bubble for 45 to 60 minutes. When rice is no longer crunchy, but easy to chew and not soggy, it is done. Onions, herbs, and spices can be added during the last 15 to 20 minutes of cooking time. Keep pot fully covered while rice is cooking, but it won't hurt to peek!

Wild Rice—This is one of the few main-dish grains that sometimes requires soaking before cooking. Wash and then soak 1 cup rice in 2 cups water and let it sit 2 to 4 hours. Only by experimentation can one determine if rice needs pre-soaking. Many varieities can just be cooked, but if they are still hard after 1 to 1½ hours, turn the heat off, let them sit until they cool and then cook them again until tender. Next time—pre-soak if using the same wild rice! Then cook same as brown rice for about 60 minutes or more. Wild rice is very expensive and rich tasting, so it is usually mixed with brown rice. This makes a more delicious, more light-tasting, less expensive dish. Cook the two rices separately and mix before serving, or cook wild rice for 15 to 20 minutes and then add brown rice to it and cook together for another 45 to 60 minutes. Add extra water if needed.

Natural Buckwheat and Pot Barley—Use about 2 cups water per 1 cup grain. Bring grain to a boil, then turn down heat to a low bubble. Cook onions with the grain and add herbs and salt for the last 10 minutes of cooking time. Cook grain 20 to 30 minutes or until no longer crunchy. Add extra water if needed.

Kasha (Toasted Buckwheat)—Cook the same as natural buckwheat for only 15 to 25 minutes. Use a bit less water for cooking.

Millet (Main Dish)—Cook the same as rice, but use 2½ cups water per 1 cup dry millet. It usually does not need pre-washing. Cooks in 40 to 55 minutes. Serve like rice and use interchangeably with rice in recipes calling for rice. This is the best of grains, highest in vitamins and very alkaline.

Whole Oats or Whole Wheat Kernals (Berries)—These must be soaked in 2½ cups of water per 1 cup grain for several hours or overnight before cooking. Then change the water and cook for about 45 to 60 minutes. They will still be slightly chewy, but not crunchy when done. This grain can be cooked separately or together with other whole grains.

Whole Rye—Soak and cook this the same as oats above, but use it sparingly because it is strong and bitter. Mix it with oats and cook them together using only 1/6th to 1/10th part rye. Rye adds zest to simple meals, but its flavour does not appeal to everyone.

STAGE I RECIPES

ALSO FOR USE IN STAGES
II and III

BEVERAGES

Lemon Drink
1 cup of water
Juice of one lemon
Several dashes of cayenne red pepper
Optional: 1–2 tsp. honey, maple syrup or molasses (The later is
　best for those with low blood sugar or diabetes.)

Mix the sweetening with the water and heat it just enough so the
sweetening will dissolve. Remove from heat and add the remaining
ingredients and serve warm *or* Chill the water and sweetening, then
add the juice and cayenne and drink.

Lemon Drink with Ginger
Using the above ingredients, simmer 1–2 tsp. of finely grated
ginger in one cup of water for about 6 minutes. Then strain and add
sweetening if desired while it's still hot. Then chill or serve warm
with the added juice and cayenne. (A large batch may be made for
each week and refrigerated. Make sure to add the lemon juice and
cayenne to it fresh daily though.)

Green Drink
6–8 leaves of green leafy vegetables (spinach, chard, mustard,
　parsley, etc.)
½ cup spring or distilled water (if possible) or regular water

Blend thoroughly and strain and drink for lots of chloryphyll and vitamins. Drink no more than ½ cup per day. ½ tsp. or more barley green powder may be used in carrot juice or with other greens as a variation.

Herb & Oil Dressing (Lemon-Oil Dressing)
(For Meat Meals)

1¼ cups oil
1–3 Tbsp. lemon juice (fresh)
1–2 tsp. wheat-free tamari soy sauce OR 1 tsp. sea salt
1 tsp. each: parsley and paprika
½ tsp. basil
¼ tsp. each: marjoram, thyme and kelp
Several dashes cayenne red pepper
Optional: ½–1 tsp. vegetable broth powder *or* onion powder

Mix together all the ingredients and beat well. Refrigerate for a couple hours so the herbs and flavours can mingle. Serve chilled or at room temperature on salads.

Herb & Oil Dressing with Garlic
(For Starchy Meals)

Eliminate the lemon juice and add 1–2 cloves of fresh crushed garlic to the above recipe.

Blended Lemon-Oil Dressing with Garlic
(For Meat Meals)

1 cup oil
2–4 Tbsp. lemon juice (fresh)
2–3 cloves garlic—minced
¼ cup fresh parsley—chopped

½ tsp. sea salt
Several dashes each: cayenne red pepper and kelp
Optional: ½ tsp. of one or more of the following: dill weed, oregano and/or basil

Blend, chill and serve. (A food processor may also be used.)

Cucumber Dill Dressing
(Makes about 1½ cups)

1 large cucumber—peeled and seeded
2 tsp. dill weed
½ cup oil (water may be used instead with some loss of flavour)
Few dashes of kelp
Several dashes of cayenne red pepper
Sea salt to taste
Optional: 1–2 cloves garlic—crushed

Blend all ingredients well, chill and serve. Best used within 5 days. Great dressing with any meal in Stage I or on:

Avocado Dressing
(Makes about 1 cup)

2 medium avocados
3–4 tsp. fresh parsley—chopped
½ cup green onion tops—chopped
½ cup oil (or ¼ cup water & ¼ cup lemon juice for meat meals)
⅛–¼ tsp. sea salt
Few dashes of kelp
Cayenne red pepper to taste

Blend all ingredients well and serve. Best used within 3 days. Good for any *Stage I meal* OR if lemon juice is used, only use with meat meals in *Stage I or II*, anytime for *Stage III*.

Romaine Salad
(Serves 2)

6–8 leaves romaine lettuce (or other lettuce except crisp-
    head)—torn in bite size pieces
1–2 stalks celery—chopped thin
1 small turnip, parsnip or new potato—grated very fine
½ cup red cabbage—shredded very fine *OR* 1 red bell pepper—in
    thin strips
Optional: green onions or chives—chopped

Wash, dry, chop and mix all ingredients. Toss and serve with a fa-
vorite dressing.

Spinach Salad
(Serves 2)

1 small or medium bunch spinach—torn
1 large beet or carrot—grated
1 zucchini—if small, slice in rounds, if larger use ½, quarter & chop
1 large avocado—in thin wedges or chunks
Optional: *Starchy Meal*—1–2 Tbsp. sunflower seeds—pre-soaked
            Meat Meal—1–2 Tbsp. raw, sliced almonds—unsoaked

Wash the spinach by swishing it in cold water to remove the sand.
Remove the stems, dry it and tear it into bite-sized pices. Scrub the
beet or carrot and zucchini and grate and chop. The sunflower seeds
should be soaked in water 1–2 hours, then drained to soften them
and make them easier to digest. Mix all the ingredients and toss
lightly. Be gentle with the spinach as it bruises and spoils easily with
too much handling or squeezing. Use lemon juice, *Lemon-Oil, Herb
& Oil, Cucumber or Avocado Dressing* depending on the type of
meal.

Zucchini Salad
(Serves 2)

2 small *or* 1 large zucchini—grated
½ regular *or* ¼ English cucumber—grated
8–12 red radishes—sliced in paper thin rounds (if none, used sliced
    carrot)
1 green bell pepper—cut in ¼ inch strips
1 leaf of lettuce (any kind but crisp-head)—torn very small
Optional: 1–2 floweret(s) of cauliflower—grated
Optional: 1–2 green onions *or* chives—chopped

Wash, dry, chop, grate and toss all ingredients. This lovely salad is
suprisingly light and delicious! Serve with dressing.

Super Sprout Salad
(Serves 2)

1 cup alfalfa sprouts
½ cup other sprouts
1 avocado—chopped
6–8 spinach leaves—torn small
½ red bell pepper—chopped small
¼ cup or less broccoli flowerets—bud tips only, break very small

Prepare and toss gently and serve. Tastes great with a tahini or
cashew-nut or *Cucumber or Avocado Dressing.*

Greek Salad
(Serves 2)

1 small cucumber—cut in chunks
1 red bell pepper (instead of tomato)—cut in chunks
½–¾ cup black olives—cut in half lengthwise
Optional: 1 small white or red onion—chopped small
Lemon-Oil Dressing OR Herb & Oil Dressing

Wash and peel the cucumber with a potato peeler (if waxed) and chop. Mix with the other ingredients and dressing, toss and refrigerate for 30–60 minutes before serving. Stir every 10–15 minutes while it marinates.

Oriental Salad
(Serves 2)

8–10 stalks asparagus—pre-steamed 10–15 min. until tender
10–14 snow peas (edible pea pods)—pull ends and top string off
1 small carrot—cut in shoe strings (see below)
1 stalk celery—cut in shoe strings
½ can bamboo shoots—rinsed and dried
½ can water chestnuts—sliced thin
Starchy Meal: add 1–2 Tbsp. raw or toasted sesame seeds
Meat Meal: add 1–2 Tbsp. home roasted (or raw) sliced almonds
Optional: green onions or chives—chopped

Prepare salad and marinate 1–2 hours before serving in fresh lemon juice *OR Lemon-Oil Dressing OR Herb & Oil Dressing.* To cut into shoe strings, chop vegetable into 2½ inch lengths. Then slice into very thin, long sticks. To roast raw almonds: Heat in a dry pan in a toaster oven at 400° for 10 minutes, until some of them pop and they are lightly browned. Use 425°–450° in a regular oven. This salad is especially nice when it is arranged artistically on a plate.

Beet Treat
(Serves 1–2)

1–3 grated beets
1–2 lemons—juiced

Mix beets and juice together and serve on a lettuce leaf or in or around an avocado half. Delicious! The lemon juice makes the beets taste sweet.

Beet Treat Salad
(Serves 2)

2–4 beets—grated (keep separate)
1 avocado—chopped
6–8 lettuce leaves (leaf, red, bibb or boston)—torn
1 green bell pepper—in rings, sliced
¼–½ cup lentil, mung, alfalfa or other sprouts

Prepare and toss all the ingredients together except the beet. Dish out the salad and spread the beets over the top. Use lemon juice or *Lemon-Oil Dressing*.

Rice Salad
(For Starchy Meals Only)
(Serves 2–3)

Use the *Spinach, Wild* or *Romaine Salad* as a base. Add ½–¾ cup pre-cooked, cold, brown rice and toss. (Fluffy, cooked millet may be used instead of rice.) Serve with a starchy meal type of dressing. *Cucumber, Avocado* or Tahini *Dressings* are suggested.

Wild Salad
(Serves 2)

Note: Please be aware of *what* you are picking and eating. Get experienced advice. Some wild plants are poisonous. Never pick salad greens from lawns or highly cultivated areas. Choose a wild, unpolluted area.

2–3 cups salad greens—may include: lamb's quarters, young & small dandelion greens, sorrels, fiddleheads, young-wild strawberry or raspberry leaves (vit. C)
8–16 wild mint leaves—torn

16–30 flower heads—(for colour & vit. C) may include: wild-purple violet blooms, blue-pea vetch blooms, white or red wild clover blooms, and/or pink-wild rose petals (petals only)

Sort and wash all leaves and flowers. Dry gently. Tear leaves for salads. Toss everything together and serve with lemon juice OR *Lemon-Oil OR Herb & Oil Dressing.*

VEGETABLES

Artichokes (Globe)

Choose firm, dark green (with no purple or 'fuzz'), well-rounded, unwrinkled artichokes. Wash 1–2 and cut off all the stalk except for about ¼ inch. Pull off and discard the first row of leaves around the stalk. With a sharp, serrated knife, cut ¾–1 inch completely off the tip end of the artichoke and discard. Snip ¼–½ inch off the tips of each remaining whole leaf. Place the vegetables upside down (top down, stalk up) in a vegetable steamer (over low boiling water) and steam for 30–40 minutes until very tender. When a knife pokes in and out easily it should be done.

Melt some butter for dipping the leaves into. Starting with the bottom row of leaves nearest and stalk, pull off one leaf at a time and dip it in the butter. With the inner part of the leaf facing upwards, pull the base of the leaf between your teeth, pulling off all tender, easy-to-chew parts. (The easy parts are the edible parts.) Discard the rest of each leaf. As you get closer to the center, you can eat more of each leaf as it keeps getting more tender until you reach the 'choke' which is a stringy, kind of prickly part that you scrape off with a spoon and discard. What's left over is *entirely* edible. Dip it in butter and savour the best part—the 'heart.' A delectable treat, and good for the liver too! For *Stage III, Citrus Butter* may be used.

Baked Turnips
(Serves 2)

Choose firm, bright coloured, white/purple turnips. Scrub 2–3 medium turnips with a good scrub brush and cut off the tip root and the stem end. Slice in ¼ inch rounds and bake on a lightly oiled baking sheet about ¼ inch apart. Bake at about 400° for 9–14 minutes until very tender, but not dry. Delicious plain or see below.

Herb Baked Turnips
(Serves 2–3)

3–4 medium turnips—sliced ¼ inch thick
¼ cup oil
1 tsp. dried parsley—crushed
½ tsp. dried basil—crushed
⅛–¼ tsp. sea salt
Few dashes each: cayenne red pepper and kelp

Mix all ingredients together well (except the turnips.) Dip the turnip slices in the mixture and bake as above.

Cinnamon Baked Squash
(1 Squash Serves 2–4)

1 Butternut, buttercup or acorn squash
Water
Cinnamon

Cut one squash in half lengthwise and scoop out and discard all the seeds. Fill the hollowed out section with water and sprinkle the entire squash generously with cinnamon. Place each half in a bread or loaf pan (to help it stay upright) with 1 inch of water in the bottom of the pan to keep the squash moist. Prick the squash all over the top surface with a knife to speed its cooking time. Bake at 400° for about 60–70 minutes until tender and a knife goes in and out easily. Serve hot with added sea salt and butter if desired. Butternut squash is naturally sweet and less stringy than the other varieties. It is beige and kind of pear-shaped, though much larger.

Honey Baked Squash
(Stage III only)

1 Squash (as above)
Water
Honey (or maple syrup)
Butter
Sea Salt

Prepare as above only fill the hollowed out section of the squash with sweetening and butter and sprinkle the entire squash with sea salt. Bake as above in water. Use the honey-butter sauce from the hollow of the squash to baste the squash with when serving. Added cinnamon is optional.

Vegetable Soup
(Serves 6–8)

6 cups water or stock
1 cup peas or chopped green beans
1 cup corn
1–2 potatoes—unpeeled, small and cubed
2–3 stalks of celery or 1 green bell pepper—chopped
2 carrots—sliced thin
1 large onion—chopped small
1 small zucchini—sliced thin or chopped
Optional: 1 stalk broccoli—chopped small

1–2 Tbsp. oil
1 Tbsp. wheat-free tamari soy sauce
3–4 tsp. vegetable broth powder OR 3–4 vegetable boullion cubes
2 tsp. parsley

1½ tsp. sea salt
½ tsp. each: basil, oregano and kelp
Several dashes cayenne red pepper
Optional: bit of honey
Optional: dark miso—keep separate

Steam the hard vegetables like potatoes and carrots for 10 minutes before making the soup. Saute the onions in the oil in a large pot until the onions are slightly transparent. Then add the water, steamed vegetables, and all the rest of the ingredients. Cook the soup on a low-to-medium heat for 40–60 minutes until all the vegetables are tender but not soggy and the flavours develop. Then take 1–2 cups of water with vegetables from the soup and blend it or use a food processor to liquify and add it back into the soup. This adds flavour and depth and gives the soup a natural thickness. Correct the soup's spices according to personal taste and add a bit of honey to balance flavours if needed, or extra water to thin the soup. After the soup is finished cooking, 1–2 Tbsp. miso can also be added to one cup of the broth and then to the soup for more taste and nutrients. Serve the soup hot and let it cool before refrigerating leftovers.

Miso Soup
(Serves 4–8)

6 cups water or stock
4–6 oz. seaweed (wakame or kombu is best)
1 large onion—chopped
2 carrots—sliced thin
2–3 stalks celery—chopped
1–2 vegetable bouillion cubes OR 1–2 tsp. vegetable broth powder
1–2 Tbsp. oil
1 tsp. parsley
½ tsp. sea salt
Several dashes kelp

⅓ cup dark miso

Saute the onions and vegetables in the oil in a large pot. Use a pot big enough to hold all the soup. When the vegetables are tender and slightly transparent, add the water, seaweed and all the rest of the soup ingredients except the miso. Let the soup cook on low heat and keep it covered and hot. Remove 1 cup of broth from the soup and mix it with the miso. When the miso is dissolved into the broth, mix it with the rest of the soup and let the soup sit covered about 5–10 minutes so the flavours can mingle. Do not cook the miso; that would destroy valuable vitamins and enzymes. Serve the soup immediately when ready. Leftover soup can be reheated slightly, but never let the soup come to a boil.

Vegetable Broth

Use 1–2 cups leftover *Miso* or *Vegetable Soup* and liquify in a blender or food processor. Add extra leftover steamed vegetables if desired. Add extra water to thin the broth to a desired consistency. Add additional flavourings if needed. Heat on low-medium heat for 15–30 minutes and serve hot or cold in a bowl or in a glass.

Carrot Soup
(Serves 4)

4 cups carrots—sliced and steamed until tender
1 1⅔ cups water or vegetable stock
2–3 Tbsp. butter 2or 1–2 Tbsp. oil (for flavour)
2 Tbsp. wheat-free tamari soy sauce
2 tsp. parsley
1 tsp. dill weed
½ tsp. sea salt
Several dashes of kelp
Cayenne red pepper to taste
Optional: several dashes of onion or garlic powder *or* a few crushed
    mint leaves

Liquify all ingredients until smooth in a blender or food processor. Then heat the soup in a saucepan on low-to-medium heat just up until a boil. Do not boil. Serve hot. Garnish with chopped chives or green onions or fresh parsley if desired.

Lentil Soup
(Serves 4)

4 cups water or stock
1 cup brown lentils
4–6 stalks celery (or broccoli)—chopped
2 carrots—sliced
1 large onion—chopped
1–2 cloves garlic—minced
2 Tbsp. butter or oil
2 Tbsp. wheat-free tamari soy sauce
3 tsp. parsley
1 tsp. sea salt
½ tsp. each: basil, oregano and thyme
⅛ tsp. cayenne red pepper
Several dashes of kelp
Optional: ½ tsp. dill weed

Bring the lentils, vegetables and water or stock to a boil on high heat, then simmer for 1 hour on low heat or until the lentils are very tender. Add the remaining ingredients and simmer another 15–20 minutes, stirring occasionally. Serve hot and enjoy. Keeps 7 days in the refrigerator or may be frozen for later use.

Split Pea Soup
(Serves 8–10)

1 lb. (2¼–2½ cups) green split peas
7–9 cups water or vegetable stock
2 medium onions—chopped small
¼ cup oil or butter

3–5 tsp. wheat-free tamari soy sauce
2 tsp. parsley
1½ tsp. sea salt
1–2 tsp. honey (to balance out the flavours)
1 tsp. each: basil, oregano and mint leaves
½ tsp. each: thyme and kelp
¼ tsp. each: marjoram and savory
Several dashes cayenne red pepper to taste
Optional: 1–2 potatoes and/or carrots—chopped small and presteamed

Cook the split peas and water in a large pot for about 1½ to 1¾ hours on medium heat or until the peas totally dissolve into the liquid. Then add the onions, herbs and vegetables and cook over a medium-to-low heat for about 20–25 minutes more to develop the flavours. Stir the soup occasionally, keeping the heat low so it does not stick or burn, just simmers. Each bowl may be topped with a bit of chopped green onion or a small handful of alfalfa sprouts.

Kidney Bean Stew
(Serves 10–12)

1 lb. dry kidney beans—soaked
1 lb. (6–10) carrots—sliced in ⅓–½ inch pieces
1 small or medium eggplant—chopped in ½–¾ inch chunks
8–20 stalks celery—chopped in ⅛–½ inch pieces
6–8 medium potatoes—in one inch chunks (leave the skins on)
3–4 medium onions—chopped
2–3 green peppers—in chunks
Optional: 6–10 jerusalem artichokes—chopped
Optional: 1–2 cups fresh or frozen corn and/or peas

2–3 Tbsp. wheat-free tamari soy sauce
1–2 Tbsp. vegetable broth powder OR 2–4 vegetable bouillon cubes
1 Tbsp. parsley
1½ tsp. sea salt
1 tsp. each: sea kelp and basil

½ tsp. paprika
⅛ tsp. or less cayenne red pepper
Optional: ⅛ tsp. cumin powder OR dill weed

Drain the soaking water from the beans and discard. Wash the beans thoroughly and cover 1 inch above them in water. (See "How to Cook Beans.") Cook the kidney beans until tender. Pour off and save all the cooking juice from the beans except for 2 cups. (Save extra juice for *Vegetarian Gravy*!) Leave 2 cups of juice with the beans.

While the beans are still cooking and nearly finished, in a separate pot steam the hard vegetables like potatoes, artichokes, carrots and eggplant for 10–15 minutes. Then add the rest of the vegetables to the hard vegetables and cook them together for another 7–10 minutes until the vegetables are tender, but still slightly crunchy.

Then add all the drained vegetables to the beans along with all the herbs and spices. (Save the steaming water for stock or *Vegetable Broth*.) Simmer everything together on low to medium heat for 20–30 minutes until the flavours mingle.

Stir-Fry Vegetables
(Serves 2–4)

½ head or less Chinese cabbage—chopped fine OR regular white or
    savoy cabbage may be used
4 stalks celery *or* bok choy—¼ inch thick, sliced on a long slant
2–4 green onions—chopped in small slanted pieces
1–2 carrots—⅛ inch thick, sliced on a long slant
1 green pepper *or* 1 stalk broccoli—chopped in long thin pieces
1–2 cloves garlic—sliced or minced
¼ cup stock, water or broth—cool
¼–⅓ cup tamari soy sauce (wheat-free)
3 Tbsp. oil—use toasted sesame oil if available
3 tsp. arrowroot powder
1–3 tsp. ginger root—peeled and finely grated

Optional: 1 cup edible pea pods and/or large, white mung bean sprouts and/or a few sliced water chestnuts

An oriental wok is preferred for this recipe, but a frying pan can be used instead. Slowly heat the oil in the wok with the garlic and be sure the sides of the wok are oiled. Add all the vegetables and ginger except for the pea pods and sprouts and cook until almost tender. Stir the mixture continuously to coat and cook the vegetables completely. Add the remaining vegetables and continue to stir.

Separately mix together well: 3 tsp. of arrowroot with ¼ cup liquid as suggested. Then mix it all together with the vegetables, heat everything another minute or two, add the tamari and perhaps several dashes of cayenne red pepper, stir and serve. Meats or tofu can be added to the stir-fry *or* it may be served over hot, whole grains like brown rice.

Shish Kebabs
(Serves Any Amount)

Use ½ – ¾ inch thick pieces about 1 to 1½ inches long of several of the following vegetables and foods: (Use about 2 – 3 cups per person.)
Pineapple chunks
Green pepper
Red bell peppers
Zucchini
Onions
Broccoli (pre-steamed 5 minutes)
Cauliflower (pre-steamed 5 minutes)
Tofu or marinated tofu
Baby shrimp
Chicken or turkey pieces (pre-cooked)

Use 2 or more skewers about 1 foot long for each person. Bamboo (from an Oriental store) or stainless steel skewers (spears) may be used. Use a variety of vegetables and other foods. Place the foods on the spears alternately, filling each spear completely. Place the skewers in a long flat baking pan with ½ inch high edges, with 2 cups of water in the bottom of the pan. Pour tamari soy sauce (wheat-free) generously over each kebab before placing right under the hot broiler of your oven. Broil 5–12 minutes, depending on the type of oven, until tender and juicy and well-browned. Serve immediately before they cool.

Bean Tacos
(Serves 6 or More)

1 dozen taco shells *or* corn tortillas *or* round rice wrappers (from Chinese stores)
Use some of the following:
Lettuce or spinach—shredded
Sprouts, any kind, alfalfa are best
Green onions or chives—chopped
Black olives—sliced
Green or red bell peppers—chopped
Cucumber—chopped
Avocado—chopped
Taco Beans (See Recipe)
Optional: Guacamole

Heat oven to 350° and place the corn tortillas on the oven racks separately for 1–2 minutes until they are firm but not brittle. Corn tortillas should be taken directly from the freezer (if frozen) and separated with a butter knife and placed right away in the oven to avoid the edges curling up. Cover each corn tortilla (or shell) with a layer of Taco Beans, assorted chopped vegetables and guacamole. If using a tortilla, eat it like a tostada (or pizza—flat) and enjoy. (If rice wrappers are used, dip them for a few seconds in hot water before filling with *hot* taco beans and vegetables. They may be wrapped and baked if desired.)

The Beans
2 cups dry pinto beans—soaked and cooked
1–2 onions—chopped

2–3 Tbsp. tamari soy sauce (wheat-free)
1 tsp. each: paprika and cumin and sea salt
½ tsp. oregano
¼ tsp. or less cayenne red pepper
⅛ tsp. each: coriander and ground cloves
Several dashes of kelp
Optional: a bit of sweetening to mellow the flavours

Cook the pinto beans until tender. Add the onions and cook another 15 minutes. Drain and save most of the water from the beans. While the beans are still hot, mix in all the herbs and spices. Mash about half the beans (leave some whole but do not separate them) with a masher or fork with a little of the drained liquid from the beans. Discard the rest of the liquid or save for other recipes or soup stock. Use the beans hot for Bean Tacos. They can also be used cold on tortillas, by spreading them on warm tortillas with some vegetables and heating under the broiler until hot, then topping with guacamole after.
In *Stage III*, sour cream may also be added.

Guacamole

1 large, ripe avocado—peeled and mashed
1 tsp. onion—crushed or minced or powder
½ tsp. paprika
Several dashes each: cayenne red pepper, cumin and kelp
Few drops of wheat-free tamari soy sauce
Vegetable salt to taste
Optional: 3–4 tsp. fresh lemon juice (*Stage II and III*)
Optional: 4–6 black olives—chopped fine

Mix the ingredients together and chill ½ hour before using to keep it fresh. Use on Bean Tacos or as a cracker or vegetable dip. (Lemon juice may be used by Stage I if the Guacamole is used as a vegetable dip for snacks. If used for a dip, bury the avocado pit in the bottom of the dip bowl to help keep the dip fresher longer!

Stuffed Green Peppers
(Serves 4–6)

1 cup dry brown rice or millet
4–6 green peppers—cut in half lengthwise and seeded
2 large or 4 small carrots—minced very small or grated
2 medium onions—chopped small
2 tsp. parsley
1 tsp. sea salt
½ tsp. each: basil, oregano and paprika
⅛ tsp. each: marjoram, thyme and kelp
1–2 Tbsp. sesame seeds *or* chopped sunflower seeds
Several dashes cayenne red pepper
1–2 Tbsp. oil

Cook the brown rice or millet for 50–60 minutes until the grain is tender and fairly dry. In a large skillet heat 1–2 Tbsp. oil and saute the onions and carrots and all the herbs until they are slightly tender. Then add the cooked grain to the skillet and saute for 5 minutes more so the flavours can mingle. Place the raw green peppers in a large uncovered baking dish (about 1½ inch sides), but side up. Fill the pepper shells with the grain-vegetable mixture. Fill the bottom of the baking dish around the peppers with about ⅓ inch of water. Bake the peppers at about 350° for 15–25 minutes until the grain is lightly browned and the peppers are tender but still a little crisp. Serve hot with *Vegetarian Gravy* or *Arrowroot Sauce* in a pinch. A half cup pre-cooked chick peas may sometimes be added to the grain in the frying pan if desired for added nutrition.

Vegetarian Gravy
2 cups kidney bean cooking juice
3 Tbsp. wheat-free tamari soy sauce
1 Tbsp. oil
2 Tbsp. arrowroot powder
½ cup millet, rice or oat flour (*Stage II or III* whole wheat may be
  used)

¼ – ½ tsp. of *one* of the following: curry powder or vegetable broth
    powder (*Stage III*, chili powder is optional)
¼ tsp. each: sea salt and kelp
Cayenne red pepper to taste

Cook ½ – 1 pounds of kidney beans and drain off and save all the liquid, or use leftover liquid from the *Kidney Bean Stew*. Use 2 cups of the "muddiest" part of the liquid for this recipe. Use the beans in another recipe or freeze them for later use. Mix all the ingredients together and stir over medium-low heat until thickened. Correct herbs and spices according to your own taste and use the gravy on *Stuffed Green Peppers*, burgers, rice, vegetables and in other recipes as desired. A wonderful gravy to use often.

Cold Bean Balls or Pate
(Serves 2–4)

1 cup pre-cooked beans — mashed (chick peas, pinto, aduki or
    kidney beans)
1 cup steamed vegetables — mashed (carrots, broccoli, zucchini or
    greens)
2 Tbsp. sesame tahini
2–4 tsp. fresh parsley — chopped fine
2 tsp. tamari soy sauce (wheat-free)
1 tsp. each: sea salt and paprika
½ tsp. each: basil and cumin
¼ tsp. each: marjoram and thyme
⅛ – ¼ tsp. cayenne red pepper
Several dashes of kelp
Optional: Toasted sesame seeds or toasted sunflower seeds — ground

Mix all the ingredients together and shape into balls. Use 1–2 Tbsp. of arrowroot powder if needed to help keep the balls firm or shape into a small loaf and slice. Use other favourite seasonings if desired. Chill before serving or serve at room temperature. The balls or pate may be coated with ground sesame or sunflower seeds. This is a great recipe to use up leftover beans and vegetables on! Try them hot too, covered in *Vegetarian Gravy*. They may be browned in a frying pan.

Curried Red Lentils
(Serves 2–4)

3–4 cups water
1 cup red lentils
1 onion—chopped small
2 Tbsp. butter (or oil)
2–3 tsp. honey to balance flavours (maple syrup or molasses can be
    used)
2 tsp. curry powder
1 tsp. each: sea salt and turmeric
1/8–1/4 tsp. each: cayenne red pepper, cominos (ground cumin) and
    coriander
Several dashes each: cinnamon and ground cloves

Begin cooking the lentils and onions in the water. Lentils (red) will take 20–30 minutes to cook fully. Do not cook them until they fall apart, just until they are tender. About 5 minutes before the lentils are finished cooking, add the spices and butter and sweetening and cook everything together another 5–10 minutes so the flavours can mingle. Correct the spices according to your own taste. Add extra water if necessary so the legumes will be contained in sauce. Enjoy with brown rice, millet or another whole grain.

Middle Eastern Falafel Spread
(Serves 4–6)

1 cup dry chick peas (garbanzos)—soaked and cooked
1/2 cup sesame tahini
2–3 tsp. fresh onion—grated or minced fine
2 cloves garlic—crushed
2–3 tsp. wheat-free tamari soy sauce
2 tsp. each: dried parsley and cumin seeds or powder (cominos)

½–1 tsp. sea salt
½ tsp. each: oregano and celery seed
¼ tsp. kelp
⅛ tsp. coriander
⅛ tsp. or less ground cloves
⅛ tsp. or more cayenne red pepper to taste

Cook the chick peas until tender, then drain and save the liquid. While the chick peas are still very hot, mash them together with the onion and all the rest of the ingredients. Herbs and spices may be altered according to personal taste. Use the falafel spread as a sandwich spread or to stuff celery with. (Extra liquid from cooking the beans may be added to the mixture if it is too dry.) Leftover spread may be refrigerated up to 7 days or frozen. The spread is tastiest when hot.

Falafel Sandwiches

Use pocket bread, *Flatbreads* or sliced bread and spread the falafel spread on one piece, topping it with sliced green pepper, cucumber rounds, green onions, chopped zucchini, avocado and/or other vegetables. Top with mayonnaise and/or mustard (Try the *Super Sandwish Topping*) or *Guacamole* and the 2nd piece of bread. Enjoy!

SNACKS AND SPREADS

Soy Cashew Nuts
(Makes 2 cups)

2 cups "raw" cashew nuts—whole if possible
2 Tbsp. butter or oil
2–4 Tbsp. wheat-free tamari soy sauce
Optional: several dashes cayenne red pepper

Heat the butter or oil in a heavy frying pan; then add the nuts and saute them for a couple of minutes. Add the soy sauce and a little cayenne if desired for a zesty taste. Stir them for a few more minutes over low heat, being careful not to burn the nuts. Blanched almonds or other nuts may be used instead, but cashews have the richest flavour. Serve like mixed nuts, either hot or cold.

Spinach-Tofu Spread or Dip
(Makes 1½ cups)

2 cups spinach (firmly packed)
6–8 oz. regular, firm tofu—mashed
2 tsp. dried parsley
1–3 tsp. wheat-free tamari soy sauce
½ tsp. basil
¼ tsp. each: oregano and marjoram
Several dashes kelp
Sea salt to taste
Cayenne red pepper to taste

Use fresh, large-leafed spinach and swish it in cool water to remove the sand. Discard the tougher spinach stems. Rinse the tofu and squeeze out the excess water. Steam the spinach 8–12 minutes until tender. Place the spinach and tofu with all the herbs in a food processor with the cutting blade. Wiz until smooth. Or add a few tsps. of water and blend a few seconds on high speed in a blender, then stop and stir. Blend and stir until smooth.

Serve with cut vegetables or fill celery with it. *Carrot, broccoli, zucchini and other vegetables may be used instead of spinach.

Tofu Spread
(Makes about 2 cups)

12 oz. tofu
1–2 stalks celery or ½ green bell pepper—chopped very fine
½ red bell pepper—chopped very fine
1 bunch of green onions (green part only) or chives—chopped very fine
¼–½ tsp. garlic powder

¼ tsp. paprika
Several dashes cayenne red pepper and kelp
Vegetable sea salt to taste

Wash and drain the tofu and mash it together with all the herbs and spices. Then mix in the remaining vegetables. Serve with vegetable sticks or stuff it in celery or ½ green pepper for elegant serving. (Mayonnaise may be added if desired.)

EGGS AND MEAT

Herbed Scrambled Eggs
(Serves 2)

6 eggs
6 Tbsp. water
½ tsp. parsley
⅛ tsp. each: paprika, basil, thyme
Several dashes each: kelp, sea salt, cayenne red pepper
1 green pepper—chopped small
Oil (or butter)

Saute the green pepper in a little oil until tender. While sauteing, beat all the other ingredients together well with a wire wisk until the eggs are foamy. Add the egg mixture to the green pepper and make sure the pan is hot. Stir occasionally for about 5 minutes or so until the eggs are somewhat solid but still very tender. (Overcooked eggs become rubbery.) Serve immediately.

Egg Foo Yong
(Makes 12 small—Serves 3–4)

6 eggs—beaten until foamy
2–3 tsp. oil

1 Tbsp. wheat-free tamari soy sauce
⅛–¼ tsp. sea salt
⅛ tsp. paprika
Several dashes of cayenne red pepper and sea kelp

6–8 oz. tofu (firm, regular type)—mashed
3–4 oz. mung bean sprouts
Optional: 2–4 oz. shredded crab or baby shrimp
Optional: ¼ cup chopped green onion tops
Extra oil for sauteing

Beat all the liquid ingredients and herbs together well. Then mix in the mashed tofu, bean sprouts and seafood if desired. Moderately oil a large skillet or griddle and heat it until fairly hot. Drop about 3–4 Tbsp. (or ¼ cup or less) of the mixture in one side of the skillet. Make 2–3 more as room permits. Fry until the bottoms are browned, about 1–3 minutes. Turn over with a metal or plastic spatula (turner) for about 1 more minute until cooked through but still tender. Re-oil the skillet for each batch.

Serve hot immediately or keep in a warmed oven until serving. Make sure to stir the mixture well before making each egg foo yong pattie. (Each pattie will be as big around as a large pancake.) Serve with egg foo yong sauce (*Arrowroot Sauce*) or wheat-free tamari soy sauce.

Arrowroot Sauce (Grain Free)
(Delicious Gravy)

1½ cups water
3 Tbsp. wheat-free tamari soy sauce
5 tsp. arrowroot powder
2 vegetable or chicken bouillion cubes OR 2 tsp. vegetable broth
   powder
Several dashes of cayenne red pepper and kelp

Mix the arrowroot thoroughly with the water in a saucepan and add the remaining ingredients. Mix well. Cook over a medium heat, stirring constantly, until thickened. Keep warm over a low heat. Keeps refrigerated up to 7 days or may be frozen.

Easy Tuna or Salmon Bake
(Serves 2–3)

1 can tuna or salmon—drained
3–4 Tbsp. mayonnaise
Vegetable salt to taste
Several dashes each: cayenne red pepper and kelp
Optional: ¼ cup green onion tops—chopped fine

Mix everything together and pat it into one or two small, oiled baking dishes about ½–⅓ inch thick. Bake at 350° for about 10–15 minutes or until browned on top. Serve immediately. Easy and delicious!

Eggsalad
(Serves 2)

4 eggs—hardboiled
2–4 tbsp. mayonnaise
⅛ tsp. paprika
Several dashes each: cayenne red pepper and kelp
Vegetable salt to taste
½ stalk celery or ¼ green pepper—minced very fine

Mash the hard-boiled eggs with the mayonnaise and spices until mashed very fine. Then add the finely chopped vegetable, mix and serve or chill for later use. Use it to stuff celery with or eat with vegetable dippers as a nutritious, high-protein snack or part of a meal.

Garlic Chicken (or Herb Baked Chicken)
(4 Pieces—Serves 2)

4 pieces chicken
3–4 Tbsp. wheat-free tamari soy sauce
4 large or 6–8 small garlic cloves
Lots of dried parsley and paprika
½ tsp. each: basil and thyme
Sea salt

Put the washed chicken in a baking dish (round, 8"–9" Pyrex suggested) with about ¼ to ⅓ inch water in the bottom. Pour the tamari over the chicken pieces. Sprinkle each chicken piece very generously with crushed, dried parsley, covering the entire surface of each piece. Next, sprinkle on just as much paprika. Sprinkle on about ⅛ tsp. each of basil and thyme over *each* piece of chicken and add sea salt as desired. Crush the garlic and place it in the water surrounding the chicken. Bake at 350°F for 30–40 minutes. After the first 10 minutes, baste the chicken with the garlic and juices from the bottom of the dish. Baste every 10 minutes until crispy and done.

Broiled Salmon or Other Fish

Wash the fish steaks or fillets and place in a Pyrex dish with about ¼–⅓ inch of water. Rub each piece with a bit of soft butter. Add a few splashes of tamari to each piece, then squeeze 1–2 tsp. of fresh lemon juice over each piece. Sprinkle with sea salt or vegetable salt, cayenne and a bit of kelp. Broil the steaks for 7–12 minutes on the first side and 3–6 minutes on the second. Broil the fillets for 3–7 minutes on the first side and 2–5 minutes on the second. Serve with butter, lemon wedges and fresh-chopped parsley.

BREADS AND MUFFINS

Sourdough Rye Bread

Starter Recipe
(Makes About 8 Cups)

In a jar with a tight fitting lid, (enough to hold 8 cups) mix 1 packet of sourdough culture with 1 cup of whole rye flour. Add ⅔ to 1 cup or so of warm water. Just enough to make a thick, stirrable batter. Cover tightly and place the jar in a warm place for 12–18 hours. Repeat this process twice more until the mixture contains 4 cups of whole rye flour and water and then let it sit for another 12–18 hours more. The mixture will then contain some bubbles and smell a bit sour. Keep the mixture refrigerated for use in recipes. It will keep for several months.

Bread Recipe
(Makes 1 Large Loaf or 2 Small)

2½ cups whole rye flour (or other Flour(s))
1–1½ cups warm water
½ cup sourdough starter
1–2 Tbsp. honey, maple syrup *or* molasses
Extra flour

Mix the warm water with the flour and sweetening and mix well. Add the starter and enough extra flour to make a stiff dough. Knead in more extra flour until the dough is no longer really sticky and does not separate. Shape it into a loaf (loaves) and place in a large, oiled loaf pan. Cover loosely with tin foil and put in a warm place for 12–18 hours. After it has doubled in size, bake it (still loosely covered in foil) at 375° for 50–60 minutes. When browned and done, let cool 10 minutes, remove from pan(s) and let *cool completely* for several hours *before* serving or wrapping for storage. This bread is more wholesome and easier to digest for those with allergies, candida or digestive problems.

Use a 'true' starter culture for sourdough breads. These are available at some health stores or order culture from:

PLAZA AMARANTHIA
Sourdough Starter - Detmold 83
P.O. Box 647, Port Coquitlam
British Columbia, Canada V3B 6H9

or

PLAZA AMARANTHIA
Sourdough Starter - Detmold 83
P.O. Box 127, Gardner
Colorado, U.S.A. 81040

Flatbreads
(A Wheat or Gluten-Free, Pita-Like Bread)
(Makes 8 Breads)

½ cup rye, barley, buckwheat, millet or amaranth flour
½ cup brown rice, oat or tapioca flour
2 tsp. arrowroot powder
½ cup water
2 tsp. oil
⅓ – ⅔ cup extra flour for kneading

Sift the flours together and keep separate. Mix the oil and water together and add to the dry ingredients. Work it together with a fork and then with your hands. Knead a bit and roll into a ball. Divide into 8 parts. Roll each in a ball and pat flat. Use a rolling pin and extra flour and roll each bread between 2 sheets of waxed paper. Turn over frequently while rolling and use enough flour so the dough does not stick. Lightly oil a frying pan and heat fairly hot. pre-heat the oven to 400°F.

Put one, somewhat rounded, about ⅛ inch thick, flatbread at a time in the frying pan. heat 15–20 seconds on each side. Then put it immediately into the oven for 3 minutes on the 1st side and then turn it over for 1½–2 minutes on the 2nd side. The breads should 'puff-up' a bit in the oven, though they will not completely puff-up like traditional pita, because pita is yeasted. Re-oil the frying pan before heating each bread. A paper towel dipped in oil may be used for re-oiling. Cool the finished breads before storage in plastic bags. Breads taste great hot too!

Chick Pea Chipatis (or Lentil)
(Makes 8–10)

1 cup chick pea flour (garbanzo flour) or lentil flour
⅓ cup water
½ tsp. oil
½ tsp. sea salt

Mix everything together well and roll into one-inch balls and pat flat. Use a rolling pin to roll out pastry-like rounds of dough. Heat a lightly oiled frying pan until very hot. Then, on medium-high heat, warm each side of the round bread for 1–2 minutes on each side until warmed and slightly browned.

Serve hot or store in the refrigerator for later use, lightly toasted or cold. Chick pea flour is sometimes called chana or besan, especially in East Indian stores. These stores also sell ready-made lentil chipatis that can be heated in a moderate oven until crispy. (Approx. 350°) for about 1–2 minutes.

Applesauce
5 to 10 lbs. baking apples, Spartan and MacIntosh are best
3 to 6 Tbsp. water

Peel the apples. (Apple peels make the sauce bitter and require blending which greatly lessens the flavour and nutrients in the sauce. It is not worth using apple peel unless the apples are organic. See below.) Chop the apples in 1 inch pieces and put in a pot with a good fitting lid. Use 3 Tbsp. water (or a bit more) for every 5 lbs. of apples. Turn the heat on high for only 1 minute. Stand close by and turn the heat down low and simmer the apples for 50–60 minutes or a bit more. It depends on the amount and type of apples. Simmer until they are tender enough to mash with a small holed hand masher. Stir the apples every 10–15 minutes while cooking. Optional sweetening or cinnamon may be added in *Stage II or III* to the finished apples but they are unnecessary if the apples are not overheated, overcooked or if too much water is not added. Eat the applesauce hot or chill for eating plain or cooking with in recipes.

Organic Applesauce

Use the above recipe, but choose organic apples. Wash and cut off any blemishes on the skin, but do not peel them. Remove the cores and chop in ½–¾ inch pieces. Cook as above, cool the apples, and blend bit by bit in a blender or food processor. Add a bit of sweetening, cinnamon and a dash of sea salt if desired, in *Stage II and III* only.

Banana Bread or Muffins (Stage II or III)
(Makes 1 Large Loaf)

2 cups flour:
1 cup regular whole wheat flour *and* 1 cup whole wheat pastry flour
   OR 1½ cups regular whole wheat flour *and* ½ cup unbleached
   white flour
2 medium bananas
½ cup honey *or* ⅓ cup maple syrup
⅓–½ cup apple, peach or pear juice
¼ cup oil
4 tsp. no-alum baking powder
2 tsp. vanilla extract
¼ tsp. sea salt

Cream the oil and sweetening together. Mash the bananas separately and beat them into the oil mixture. In a separate bowl, sift all the dry ingredients together and add them to the wet mixture. Add the ⅓ cup juice and vanilla and beat well. Add extra juice only if the batter is too stiff. Scoop the mixed ingredients into an oiled and floured pan and bake at 350° for 55–65 minutes until nicely browned on top and a toothpick comes out fairly clean. Do not remove the bread from the oven while testing or until completely baked. Let the bread cool before slicing or it will be doughy. See: How to Make Muffins.

Pumpkin Bread or Muffins (Stages I or II or III)
Follow the Banana Bread recipe except for these changes:
Instead of bananas use 1 cup of cooked and mashed pumpkin
Increase the honey to 1 cup *or* maple syrup to ⅔ or ¾ cup
Add 1–1½ tsp. cinnamon
Add ⅛ tsp. each: nutmeg and ginger

Apple Raisin Bread or Muffins (Stage II or III)
Follow the Banana Bread recipe except for these changes:
Instead of bananas use 1 cup applesauce or stewed apples (peeled)
Use apple juice
Add ½–1 cup raisins
Add 1 tsp. cinnamon
Add several dashes each: nutmeg and ginger

Zucchini or Carrot Bread or Muffins (Stage I or II or III)
Follow the Banana Bread recipe except for these changes:
Instead of bananas use 1 cup of small zucchini *or* carrots—grated very fine
Increase the honey to ¾ cup *or* the maple syrup to ½ cup
For Zucchini Bread, 2 Tbsp. grated orange rind may be added
For Carrot Bread, 1 tsp. cinnamon may be added

How to Make Muffins

The above recipes make about 10–12 muffins. Fill lightly oiled and floured muffin tin cups (or use paper cup inserts for muffins) ⅔ to ¾ full of batter and bake about 25–40 minutes at 350°. Fill any leftover, empty muffin cups with water before baking. Refrigerate all homemade breads and muffins.

STAGE II RECIPES

ALSO FOR USE IN STAGE III

SALAD DRESSINGS

Yogurt Garlic Dressing
1 cup plain yogurt
1–2 cloves garlic—crushed
1–2 Tbsp. fresh lemon juice
Dash or two of sea salt
Optional: bit of cayenne red pepper

Mix together very well. Do not blend. Chill before serving.

Yogurt Dill Dressing
1 cup plain yogurt (preferably a tart variety)
2–3 tsp. dill weed (to taste)
1–3 tsp. fresh lemon juice
Optional: ¼ cup or less chives or green onion tops—chopped fine

Mix (don't blend) all ingredients together well. Add a bit of sea salt
if desired. Serve at room temperature or chilled if preferred.

Yogurt Green Onion Dressing
1 cup plain yogurt
½ cup green onions (white and green parts)—chopped
2–3 tsp. fresh parsley—chopped
1–2 tsp. tamari soy sauce
¼ tsp. each: sea salt, paprika and basil (may use fresh)

Blend all ingredients thoroughly for a better blend of flavours and a green coloured dressing. Chill before serving.

CHEESES

Buttermilk Cheese
(Makes about 1 cup)

1 litre buttermilk

Pre-heat the oven to 225°. Pour the buttermilk into a 9"×12" baking pan and bake for 1½ hours. The buttermilk will separate. Strain the "cheese" in a colander lined with cheesecloth or a fine strainer. Let it strain for about 1 hour while gently stirring the cheese every 15 minutes or so to help remove the whey. Then chill the "cheese" and use in recipes. (This makes a lovely cheese similar to cottage cheese in texture and flavour, but without the additives found in cottage cheese. J.M.M.) It keeps 1–2 weeks refrigerated.
*Original Recipe by Joyce Cherry

Cheese and Chives
1 cup buttermilk cheese
⅓ cup chopped chives or green onions (finely chopped)
1–3 tsp. fresh lemon juice
Sea salt to taste

Mix all ingredients and enjoy stuffed in celery or avocado or in *Stage II*, stuffed in a tomato.

Buttermilk Cheese Spread

Follow the recipe for the *tofu spread* but use Buttermilk Cheese instead of the tofu. Delicious!

Borscht
(Serves 8–10)

4 cups water from steamed vegetables
4 cups cabbage—shredded
2 cups beets—chopped or sliced
1 cup potatoes—chopped in small cubes
1 cup tomato puree
½ cup carrot—sliced thin (about 1 medium)
2 large onions—chopped small (about 1½–2 cups)
1½–2 Tbsp. apple cider vinegar
1½–2 Tbsp. honey (same amount as vinegar)
1 Tbsp. vegetable broth powder OR 2 vegetable bouillon cubes
1–1½ tsp. sea salt
3 bay leaves
¼ tsp. dill weed
cayenne red pepper to taste
3 Tbsp. oil or butter
Optional toppings: chopped tomatoes, or chives or fresh parsley
    and/or sour cream or yogurt

Steam the beets, potatoes and carrot until tender and save the steam-ing water. Add extra water if needed to equal 4 cups stock and put aside. In a soup pot, saute the onions in hot oil or butter until semi-tender. Add the cabbage and saute another 5–8 minutes until the cabbage is fairly tender. Add the 4 cups steamed vegetable water and the steamed beets, potatoes and carrot. Add the rest of the in-gredients (except the toppings), stir, cover and let simmer on low heat for about one half hour. Remove the bay leaves and adjust the flavour if desired. Serve hot with topping(s).

Turkey Soup
(Serves 10–16)

12–16 cups water or stock
Bones of 1 turkey
1½–2 cups turkey pices—cut small

4–6 stalks celery—chopped
2 zucchini—chopped
2 large onions—chopped
2–3 cloves garlic—minced
3 tsp. vegetable broth powder
2 vegetable bouillon cubes
4 Tbsp. tamari soy sauce
2 Tbsp. parsley
2 Tbsp. butter or oil
1–2 tsp. sea salt
1 tsp. basil
½ tsp. thyme
⅛ tsp. each: cayenne red pepper and kelp

Bring the water and turkey bones on high heat to a boil, then turn down low to medium until the water is barely bubbling and simmer for 2–4 hours to make flavourful turkey stock and draw the calcium from the bones into the water. Then strain and save the water (stock) and discard the bones, retaining any leftover, wholesome bits of meat.

Saute the onion, garlic and vegetables in the oil or butter until somewhat tender, in a large skillet and add this to the turkey stock along with the remaining ingredients. Simmer everything together for 1–2 hours. Serve or save until the next day. Soup is best the 2nd to 7th day as the flavours have developed more. Leftovers may be frozen.

Sweet and Sour Lentils
(Serves 3–4)

2 to 2½ cups water
1 cup brown lentils
1 small onion—chopped
3–4 Tbsp. apple cider vinegar
3–4 Tbsp. honey
1 Tbsp. oil

1 tsp. sea salt
1 tsp. basil

Bring the water and lentils to a boil on high heat and immediately turn the heat to low so the lentils are bubbling slightly. Cook them covered for about ½ hour, add the onions and cook another 15 minutes. After 45 minutes, if most of the water is not cooked out or absorbed by the lentils, remove the lid of the pan and let the lentils finish cooking for another 15–20 minutes until most of the liquid is gone and the lentils are fully cooked and very tender. then add the oil, seasonings, and extras and cook the lentils for another 5–8 minutes or so covered, until the flavour of the spices mingles with the lentils. When finished cooking, the lentils should look like a very thick soup or stew. Serve hot or cold. Great for lunches.

Ratatouille
(Serves 4)

1 medium eggplant—peeled and cubed
1 cup tomato juice
1 large onion—chopped small
4–6 cloves garlic—minced
¼ cup oil
2 bay leaves (remove before serving)
2 tsp. dried parsley
1½ tsp. sea salt
1 tsp. each: basil, marjoram and oregano
⅛ tsp. rosemary
Cayenne red pepper to taste

3–4 medium tomatoes—in small chunks

2 large green peppers—in strips
2 medium zucchini—in chunks
2 Tbsp. tomato paste

Optional: fresh, chopped parsley or green onions or chives

Heat the oil in a large cooking pot and saute the onion and garlic until slightly tender on fairly high heat. Add the eggplant and salt it lightly. Continue to saute until the eggplant is a bit tender and the onions and garlic are somewhat transparent. Then add the tomato juice and herbs, stir, cover and simmer on low heat for about 12–15 minutes until the eggplant is very tender. Then add the peppers and zucchini, tomatoes and tomato paste. (The tomatoes may be added earlier with the eggplant if more tender tomatoes are desired.) Stir and simmer 5–10 more minutes until the new vegetables are a bit tender but still retain a bit of crunchiness, or are as tender as you like. It can be topped with fresh parsley or green onions or chives. (*In Stage III* it may be served over rice or other grain.)

Baked Beans
(Serves 6–8)

2 cups dry white pea or navy beans
½ cup molasses
⅓ cup tomato paste
1 medium onion—chopped fine
2 Tbsp. tamari soy sauce
2 tsp. apple cider vinegar
1½ tsp. sea salt
1 tsp. each: curry powder and dry mustard
½ tsp. sea kelp

Cook the beans until tender. Drain off all the water except 1½ cups. Use the 1½ cups water to mix with the beans and remaining ingredients. Scoop the mixture into a lightly oiled 1 or 1½ quart (or litre) baking dish. Bake for 1 hour in the uncovered dish at 275°–300° and then serve. Leftovers reheat easily in a saucepan.

Broiled Tofu Burgers
(Serves 4–6)

1½–2 cups water
¼–⅓ cup tamari soy sauce, *Quick Sip* or teriyaki sauce

½ tsp. curry powder
¼ tsp. each: cayenne red pepper and cumin
Several dashes of kelp
14–16 oz. regular plain tofu—in one block

Freeze the block of tofu (packaged or in a plastic bag) overnight or until it is frozen solid. Defrost it by putting the package of tofu in hot water. When it is defrosted, remove the package, rinse the tofu and gently press out all the excess water. Slice the tofu into slabs about ½ inch thick.

Simmer the tofu slices in the marinade for 15–20 minutes. Then drain the tofu slices and broil them for 2–3 minutes on each side before serving with *Super Sandwich Topping* or plain mustard or another topping. Enjoy it with a hearty salad or steamed or sauteed vegetables.

Spanish Omelet
(Serves 1–2)

4 eggs—separate yolks and whites
4 Tbsp. hot water
½ tsp. sea salt
⅛ tsp. paprika
Several dashes cayenne red pepper
2 tsp. butter (or oil)
1 batch of Spanish Sauce (kept hot)

Beat the egg whites until stiff and peaks are formed. Set aside. Beat the yolks thoroughly until foamy. Melt the butter in a hot omelet pan while heating the broiler in the oven. Mix the water, sea salt, paprika and cayenne with the egg yolks. Then slowly fold the stiff egg whites into the yolk mixture. Pour the eggs into the hot buttered pan and cook, unstirred on medium heat until the omelet sets and is brown underneath. Then place the pan under the broiler to brown the top of the omelet. After it begins to brown, put 2–3 spoonfuls of the Spanish Sauce in the centre of the omelet and fold it over. Finish cooking the omelet 1–2 more minutes if needed, then serve it topped with the rest of the Spanish Sauce.

Spanish Sauce

2 Tbsp. butter
1–2 green onions—chopped
8–10 black olives—sliced
½ green pepper—chopped small
4–6 mushrooms—sliced OR ¼ cup eggplant—pre-cooked & finely
  chopped
¼ tsp. each: sea salt, dried & crushed red peppers, and paprika
Cayenne red pepper to taste
2 cups tomatoes—seeded and chopped

Melt the butter in a saucepan and saute the onion and green pepper
until fairly tender. Add the tomatoes and simmer uncovered for
12–20 minutes until they are very tender and have broken apart and
much of the liquid from the tomatoes has evaporated. Add the rest
of the ingredients, simmer another 5 minutes covered and use according to the omelet recipe to fill and cover the omelet or serve the
sauce over brown rice or another whole grain in *Stage III* only.

Super Sandwich Topping

1 Tbsp. mayonnaise
1 Tbsp. grey mustard
Several dashes each: cayenne red pepper and kelp
Optionals: ½ tsp. miso *or* tamari soy sauce
Optionals: ⅛–¼ tsp. vegetable salt *or* onion or garlic powder

Mix everything together well and use as a spread on *Tofu Burgers,
Falafel Sandwiches,* Vegetable Sandwiches and others. Adds a delicious kick to any sandwich.

Shrimp Creole
(Serves 2–4)

½ cup green pepper—chopped small
½ cup green onions—chopped (white & green parts)
¼ cup celery—chopped small

1 medium carrot—diced very fine
2 Tbsp. oil
1–2 cloves garlic—minced
1 cup mushrooms—sliced OR 1 cup eggplant—diced and pre-cooked
    tender
2–3 Tbsp. fresh parsley—chopped
3 cups tomatoes (canned or fresh)—chopped
½ tsp. basil
¼ tsp. thyme
Several dashes cayenne red pepper
Optional: sea salt to taste if desired
½ lb. or 200–300 gms. fresh baby shrimp (use more if desired)

On medium-high heat, saute the onions, garlic, pepper, celery and carrot for a few minutes until somewhat tender. Add the mushrooms (or pre-cooked eggplant) and parsley and cook for 3–5 minutes more. Then add the tomatoes and herbs, stir and simmer on low heat for 30 minutes, covered. Lastly, add the shrimp, stir and simmer an additional 3–5 minutes. Serve over steamed, chopped cauliflower for *Stage II* or over brown rice, pasta or another whole grain in *Stage III*. This lovely delicate flavoured dish should be eaten the first day if possible. However, leftovers may be eaten the 2nd day or the 3rd day at the lates

PANCAKES

Amazing Amaranth Pancakes
(Grain-free)
(Makes 8 or 10 – 3 inch pancakes)

1 egg, beaten
¼ cup apple juice*
1 tsp. oil
¼ cup amaranth flour
¼ cup tapioca flour

3 Tbsp. arrowroot powder
¼ tsp. cinnamon
¼ tsp. baking powder (wheat-free)
⅛ tsp. sea salt

Beat the egg until light and foamy. Mix in the juice and oil. Lightly oil a frying pan and heat it until very hot. Lower the heat to medium high. While the pan is warming add the remaining dry ingredients one by one and beat thoroughly. Once the batter is ready, make the pancakes immediately. Use 2–3 Tbsp. batter per pancake and keep the pan hot. Once the bottom browns, flip the pancakes over. Watch carefully as the pancakes cook quickly. Lightly re-oil the frying pan with a napkin or paper towel *before* each new batch.

*Other sweet fruit juices may be used instead of apple, such as: mango, papaya, peach, pear or apricot.

Millet and/or Rice Pancakes
(Gluten-free)

1 egg, beaten
1½ cups milk substitute
1 cup millet flour*
1 cup brown rice flour*
½ cup tapioca flour
Several dashes of sea salt

Follow the directions for AMAZING AMARANTH PANCAKES. These make light, thin pancakes. To thicken add ¼ cup extra flour (your choice) and/or ¼ tsp. baking powder.

*Instead of 1 cup each millet and brown rice flour, 2 cups of millet *or* brown rice flour may be used. Makes about 1½–2 dozen—3 inch pancakes.

Buckwheat Pancakes
(Wheat-free)

2 eggs, beaten
1–1¼ cup milk substitute*
1½ cups millet or brown rice flour
¾ cup buckwheat flour
Several dashes sea salt
Optional: ¼ tsp. cinnamon

Follow directions for the *AMAZING AMARANTH PANCAKES*. *A sweet fruit juice may be used instead of milk substitute. If desired, try: apple, apricot, peach, pear or tropical fruit juices. Makes about 1½–2 dozen—3 inch pancakes.

STAGE III RECIPES

DRESSINGS

Citrus Butter for Artichokes
(For 1 or 2)

¼ cup butter—melted
¼ tsp. fine grated orange rind
2 Tbsp. orange juice (fresh)
1 Tbsp. lemon juice (fresh)

Mix the rind and juices with the melted butter and serve with steamed artichokes for dipping the leaves in. *Stage III* only.

Easy Thousand Island Dressing
1 cup natural mayonnaise
1-2 Tbsp. tomato paste
2–4 tsp. apple cider vinegar *or* fresh lemon juice
⅓ cup chopped pickles *or* relish
1–2 tsp or more honey *or* maple syrup to taste
Several dashes each: sea salt and cayenne red pepper

Beat all ingredients together well and adjust the flavourings if needed. Chill before serving with *Stage III* salads.

SOUPS

Broccoli or Zucchini Soup
(Serves 3–4)

3–4 stalks broccoli (4 cups)—chopped for steaming OR 3–4
   zucchini (4 cups)—chopped
1½ cups cashew or almond milk
2–3 tsp. parsley
½ tsp. basil
¼–½ tsp. sea salt
¼ tsp. each: thyme and paprika
Several dashes cayenne red pepper

Steam the vegetables until tender, then blend them with the "milk"
and herbs. Put the soup in a saucepan and heat it just to boiling on
medium heat. (Do not boil or overheat!) Serve immediately. This is
a wonderful, creamy type soup, more flavourful than soups made
with cow's milk which actually detracts from the flavour of the vegetables.

Nut Milk
2–3 Tbsp. "raw" cashew pieces or raw blanched almonds
1½ cups water

Blend thoroughly in the blender or a food processor for 2–4 minutes
until the water becomes white with the blended nuts. (At highest
speed.) Strain and use in many recipes instead of cow's milk.

Tomato Lentil Soup
(Serves 8–10)

8 cups water or stock
2 cups lentils
13 oz. can of tomato paste

3–4 medium tomatoes—chopped OR 1 large can (28 oz. or 795 ml)
  tomatoes with juice—chopped
2–3 stalks celery—chopped
1 large onion—chopped
2–4 tsp. tamari soy sauce
2 tsp. parsley
1–2 tsp. honey (to balance the flavours)
1 tsp. each: sea salt, basil and oregano
½ tsp. each: kelp, marjoram and thyme
Several dashes cayenne red pepper

Cook the lentils and water for 30 minutes in a large pot on medium
heat. Add the onions, tomatoes, and vegetables and cook these all
together for another 30 minutes. Add the remaining ingredients and
continue cooking everything on low heat for about 20–25 minutes
or until the tomatoes have turned into liquid, the vegetables are
tender, and the lentils are very soft. Stir the soup occasionally.

Clam Chowder
(Serves 8–10)

2 cans whole baby clams with juice (approx. 5 oz. clams & 5 oz.
  juice)
2½ cups water
2 cups milk or 1½ cups milk & ½ cup cream
2–3 Tbsp. butter
1 medium onion—chopped small
3 cups potatoes—unpeeled, diced
6 Tbsp. whole wheat flour (or millet or arrowroot)
1–2 tsp. sea salt
¼ tsp. paprika
Several dashes cayenne red pepper

Carefully melt the butter (so it won't burn) in about a 1 gallon pot
and saute the onion in it until slightly tender, then add the flour and
saute until browned to add flavour. Next, add the water and potatoes

(rinse the potatoes well in cool water before adding to the soup) and simmer on low to medium heat for 15–20 minutes until the potatoes are fairly tender. Then add the clams with their juice and the spices and simmer 25 minutes more. In a small saucepan heat the milk until hot but not boiling. Add the hot milk to the soup and simmer 10 minutes more. Keep the soup covered at all times and be careful not to burn it using too high a heat. Serve and enjoy when ready. It's delicious the 1st day or the next. Keeps 5–6 days refrigerated and may be frozen if defrosted slowly.

MAIN DISHES

Lentil Burgers
(Serves 6)

2 cups dry lentils —cooked until tender and drained (see Sweet and
    Sour Lentils for how-to)
1–2 eggs —beaten foamy
1 medium onion —diced
½ cup cracker crumbs
1 tsp. tamari soy sauce
½–1 tsp. sea salt
⅛ tsp. kelp
Cayenne red pepper to taste
Tomato juice

Mix all the ingredients together and use just enough tomato juice to hold the mixture together and shape into burgers. Fry like other burgers in a skillet or on a griddle that is oiled and hot. Cook about 12–20 minutes on the first side and 6–12 on the second side, or until nicely browned. These are best served without a bun, with ketchup or a sauce or gravy. Try *Arrowroot Sauce* or *Mushroom Gravy.*

Pecan-Cheese Loaf
(Serves 8)

1½–2 cups pecans—crushed very small
1½ cups cooked brown rice
1 cup wheat germ
1 cup mushrooms—sliced thin
1¼ lbs. aged cheddar cheese—grated
1 large onion—minced
2 cloves garlic—minced or crushed
1–2 tsp. tamari soy sauce
1/16–⅛ tsp. cayenne red pepper
Several dashes kelp
4 extra large (or 5 large) eggs—beaten foamy

Combine all the ingredients except the eggs in a large bowl. Mix thoroughly, add the eggs and mix again. Pack the mixture into a heavily oiled 9″ or 10″ square baking pan. Bake at 350° for 45–50 minutes or until firm and browned. Cut into pieces and serve with hot *Mushroom Gravy*. It has a meatloaf consistency and tastes terrific!

Mushroom Gravy I
1¾ cups water
1 cup mushrooms—sliced thin
½ cup whole wheat flour (or millet)
2–3 Tbsp. tamari soy sauce
2 vegetable bouillon cubes
3 tsp. vegetable broth powder
Cayenne red pepper to taste
Several dashes kelp

Mix all the ingredients together and heat in a saucepan on medium heat, stirring constantly until very hot, then simmer on lowest heat about 15 minutes until thickened and the mushrooms are tender. Serve hot over nut loafs, burgers, grains or vegetables. Chill leftovers for later use. Delicious!

Mushroom Gravy II
1 cup milk
1 cup sliced mushrooms
1 large onion—chopped fine
1 clove garlic—minced
4 Tbsp. arrowroot powder—mixed in ¼ cup water
2 Tbsp. butter
1 Tbsp. tamari soy sauce
Sea salt to taste
Several dashes cayenne red pepper and kelp

In a saucepan saute the onions and garlic in the butter until slightly tender. Add the mushrooms and continue to saute until the onions and garlic are fairly transparent and the mushrooms are tender. Add the arrowroot mixture and stir until thickened. Then add the remaining ingredients, stir a minute or two longer and serve. Use as above.

Cauliflower Patties
(Makes and Serves 6–8)

1 cup raw cauliflower—grated
1 cup cashew pieces—crushed
1 cup medium or sharp cheddar cheese—grated
1 cup bread crumbs
1 small onion—chopped very fine
1 clove garlic—crushed
1 Tbsp. whole wheat flour
1 Tbsp. dried parsley *or* 2–3 Tbsp. fresh parsley—chopped
1 Tbsp. butter or oil
½ tsp. each: sea salt and thyme
Several dashes each: cayenne red pepper and kelp
2 extra large eggs—beaten foamy

Mix all the ingredients together except the eggs. After mixing, add the eggs and mix again. Form into patties and cook like burgers in an oiled skillet or on a griddle. In the hot pan (or griddle) broil each pattie for about 10 minutes on the first side and a bit less on the second until browned. Serve with *Mushroom Gravy*.

Spiced Vegetables and Polenta
(Serves 4–6)

1 medium eggplant—peeled and cubed
1 cup tomato juice
1 large onion—chopped small
4–6 cloves garlic—minced
¼ cup oil
1 tsp. each: cumin, ground coriander and chili powder
1½ tsp. sea salt
Hot sauce and/or Cayenne red pepper to taste
3–4 medium tomatoes—in small chunks
2 large green peppers—in strips
2 medium zucchini—in chunks
3 Tbsp. tomato paste

Optional: fresh, chopped parsley, or green onions or chives

Cook the above in exactly the *same* way as the Ratatouille. (The vegetables are the same but the herbs and spices are different.) Serve over hot Polenta as soon as prepared. Both may be reheated again if needed.

Polenta
3½–4 cups water
1½ cups whole yellow corn meal
1½ cups medium cheddar cheese—grated
1 tsp. sea salt

Mix the cold water and corn meal together in a large sauce pan and stir over medium heat until it thickens and is no longer grainy. Turn the heat down low and keep stirring while adding the cheese and sea salt. As soon as the cheese is melted the polenta is done. Scoop ½ cup or more onto a warm plate and top with the spiced vegetables. Top with parsley, green onions or chives and enjoy! A little sour cream or yogurt is also nice with this.

Gado-Gado Spicy Peanut Sauce with Vegetables
(Serves 6)

2 medium onions—chopped small
2–3 cloves garlic—minced
2 Tbsp. butter or oil
2 bay leaves (remove before serving)
2 tsp. fresh ginger root—grated fine

2–2½ cups water
1 cup natural peanut butter
¼ cup fresh lemon juice
1 Tbsp. honey
1 Tbsp. apple cider vinegar
1 tsp. tamari soy sauce
½–1 tsp. sea salt
⅛–¼ tsp. cayenne red pepper to taste

Saute the onions, garlic, bay leaves and ginger in the butter or oil until slightly tender, about 2–3 minutes. Add the remaining ingredients, mix thoroughly and simmer on the lowest possible heat for 30–35 minutes, stirring occasionally.

Serve Over:
2 cups shredded cabbage—raw or steamed
1 cup raw carrot—grated
1 cup raw celery—sliced

1 cup marinated tofu chunks
3–6 hard boiled eggs—sliced
3 Tbsp. toasted sunflower seeds or nuts

3 cups mixed steamed vegetables—broccoli, zucchini, and/or mushrooms, etc.

On one large platter, or separately on each plate, first arrange a layer of raw ingredients, then one of steamed, then the egg slices and tofu, nuts or seeds. Top with the sauce and enjoy!

Pita Pizzas
(Serves 2)

4 whole wheat pita breads
2–3 cups tomato sauce—warmed
2 cups medium cheddar, swiss or mozzarella cheese—grated
2–4 Toppings: sliced black olives, chopped green peppers, tomato slices, zucchini or mushroom slices, chopped onions, pineapple chunks, and/or chopped meats

Heat the breads in the oven for 1–2 minutes to warm them and cover them with hot tomato sauce (heated in a saucepan). Cover with toppings and broil for 1–3 minutes until hot and crispy. Enjoy these fast, easy and scrumptious pizza treats as a meal or quick snack. They are great hot and taste good cold in lunches too.

Spaghetti
Whole wheat or other whole grain noodles
Tomato sauce
Parmesan Cheese

Add the noodles to already boiling water and keep the heat just high enough so it continues to bubble (though not furiously.) Use a large cooking pot and at least 1 gallon of water per pound of noodles. Cook the noodles until tender outside and still a bit firm inside, not mushy but not chewy. Noodles may take from about 5 to 20 minutes to cook depending on the type of noodle and what it's made from. Do not always trust package instructions as they are sometimes incorrect. When ready, drain the noodles in a colander and serve immediately with tomato sauce (or other sauce) and Parmesan cheese.

Lasagne Rice
Brown rice
Tomato sauce
Medium cheddar cheese (undyed)—grated
Parmesan cheese

Cook the brown rice and during the last 10 minutes of cooking time, sprinkle the grated cheese over the rice so it can melt. When ready, serve with tomato sauce and sprinkled Parmesan cheese. Enjoy this delicious and more nutritious version of lasagne.

Confetti Rice
(Serves 2–3)

2 cups cooked brown rice—still hot (about 1 cup dry)
1 large avocado—chopped
2 medium tomatoes—chopped
½ cup mushrooms—sliced
4–5 tsp. tamari soy sauce
½ tsp. vegetable salt
½ tsp. vegetable mixed seasoning like: Spike, Herbamare, etc.
1/16 tsp. cayenne red pepper
Dash or two of kelp

Cook the brown rice and add the mushrooms on top the last 10–15 minutes of its cooking time. While the rice is still hot, mix in the raw tomato and avocado along with the herbs according to taste. Serve immediately as it cools quickly and should be eaten hot. This dish does not reheat or store well. It's best to eat fresh, right after preparing. Delicious!

Terrific Tomato Sauce
(Makes about 5 cups)

13 oz. tomato paste
1–1½ cups water

4 medium tomatoes—chopped
1 large onion—chopped small
1 small eggplant or 1 cup mushrooms—chopped
2–3 cloves garlic—minced
3 bay leaves (take out later)
2 Tbsp. tamari soy sauce
2 Tbsp. oil
2–3 tsp. parsley
2 tsp. each: basil and oregano
1 tsp. each: sea salt and honey (or maple syrup)—to balance flavours
½ tsp. each: marjoram, thyme, kelp and rosemary
⅛ tsp. or less cayenne red pepper

Heat the oil in a large pot (dutch oven) on medium-high tempera-ture. When the oil is hot, add chopped onions and garlic and egg-plant or mushrooms and saute until they are tender. Then add the tomatoes and cook until they turn to liquid. Add the tomato paste and water and mix everything together thoroughly. Lastly, add all the herbs and spices and simmer the sauce on very low heat for 40–60 minutes with the lid covering the pot, stirring occasionally. A little extra water may be added for a looser consistency. Correct the herbs and spices if needed. When the sauce is finished, remove the bay leaves. Then use the sauce in recipes or refrigerate it no longer than 7 days or freeze for later use. The recipe can be doubled or tripled for larger batches. Be sure to use less sea salt when in-creasing recipe sizes.

EGGS AND MEAT

Vegetable Quiche
(Makes 2 Pies—Serves 8–12)

Optional: 2 9" or 10" pie crust shells (see recipes)
12–16 oz. swiss cheese—grated (half cheddar may be used)
4 extra large or 5 large eggs—beaten until foamy

½ lb. mushrooms—sliced
2 cups broccoli—chopped
2 medium onions or 6–8 green onions—chopped fine
2 green peppers—chopped
2 Tbsp. oil
2 tsp. tamari soy sauce
1½ tsp. sea salt
1 tsp parsley
½ tsp. each: paprika and basil
Several dashes each: cayenne red pepper and kelp
1½ to 2 cups milk

Sauté the onions and vegetables in oil along with the sea salt and herbs. Pour off any excess liquid. When the vegetables are tender, mix them with the tamari and set them aside until the cheese sauce is ready. Heat the milk. (Use more milk if more cheese is used.) Take the milk off the heat *before* if comes to a boil and in the grated cheese.

Stir the sautéed vegetables and spread ¾ of them in the unbaked pie crust shells. (To avoid using a pie crust—just lightly oil a pie pan.) Mix the beaten eggs into the melted cheese and milk and pour-scoop them over the vegetables in the pie pan. Do not leave the cheese or eggs in the milk for more than a minute or two, or the eggs will harden and the cheese become rubbery. Top the pie with the remaining vegetables, spread out evenly over the milk mixture. Bake immediately in a pre-heated oven at 350° for 35–45 minutes or until the pie is slightly browned, golden in colour and firm. (¼–½ lb. or 100–200 gms. shredded crab or baby shrimp may be added as a variation in some quiches.)

Fish in Cream Sauce
(Serves 2–4)

1 lb. fresh or frozen fish fillets (try sole, cod, haddock, etc.), (defrost
   if frozen)
1½–2 cups milk or milk substitute
2–3 tsp. butter (or oil)

½–1 cup mushrooms—sliced
¼ tsp. each: basil and paprika
1 tsp. dried parsley
Several dashes each: sea salt, cayenne red pepper and kelp

Place the fish in a lightly oiled low-sided baking dish. (Pyrex is a good choice.) Pour the milk over the fish and around it. Then sprinkle or pour on the rest of the ingredients and place little dabs of butter on top. Broil for 7–12 minutes on the first side and 5–7 minutes on the second side, until tender but not dry. Serve with lemon wedges and/or tartar sauce.

DESSERTS

Carob Frosting
Sift together:
½ cup milk powder—non-instant is best
½ cup roasted carob powder (dark)
Optional: 2–3 tsp. instant coffee substitute (for a more chocolatey flavor)

Add:
⅓–½ cup honey
6 Tbsp. milk
2 Tbsp. light oil
1–2 tsp. vanilla
4–6 drops peppermint extract
Optional: ¼–⅓ cup coconut—shredded, unsweetened to sprinkle on top of cake

Mix the carob powder with the non-instant milk powder. Mix all the other ingredients and slowly add dry ones to them and mix thoroughly until smooth. (If noninstant milk powder is not available, mix instant milk powder separately with the milk, then add rest of the wet ingredients and mix. Lastly, add carob powder. Instant milk powder tends to stay lumpy when mixed differently. Double the frosting ingredients if lots of frosting is wanted.

Add extra milk if thinner frosting consistency is wanted. Frosting will thicken and harden as it chills. Chill frosting for 1–2 hours before using on the cake.

Carob Cake
(Makes 1—9"×13" or 1—2-layer 8" round cake)

Wet Ingredients:
1½ cups honey
1–1½ cups milk
½ cup light oil or softened butter
3 extra large eggs—beaten
2 tsp. lemon or orange rind
2 tsp. vanilla
1–2 tsp. lecithin—liquid

Dry Ingredients:
2½ cups w.w. flour—half pastry, half regular
½–⅔ cup roasted carob powder
2–4 oz. walnuts or pecans—chopped
3–4 tsp. baking powder—low or no-alum
½ tsp. salt
Optional: 1–2 Tbsp. gluten flour
Optional: 3–4 tsp. instant coffee substitute

Mix all the wet ingredients together well with a fork or wire whisk. In a separate bowl mix the dry ingredients by sifting them together once and stirring. Begin by using only 1 cup milk and add the extra ½ cup if the mixture is too dry. The mixture should be thick but able to be poured into the baking pan(s). Beat the cake batter 100–200 strokes until smooth and then mix in the nuts. Lightly oil and flour the pan(s), pour in the cake batter, and bake at 325° for 45–60 minutes until lightly browned and a toothpick comes out clean. Cool the cake before removing the cake from the pans and adding frosting. Frost with carob frosting for the best tasting cake, although cream frosting may also be used.

24 Karat (Carrot) Cake
(Makes 1—9"×13" or 1—2 or 3 layer 8" round cake)

Wet Ingredients:
6 medium carrots—grated fine (about 2 cups)
1½ cups honey
¾—1 cup milk
⅓ cup oil
3 extra large eggs—beaten
2 tsp. vanilla

Dry Ingredients:
2½ cups w.w. flour—half pastry, half regular
2—4 oz. walnuts or pecans—chopped
3—4 tsp. baking powder
1 tsp. cinnamon
½ tsp. nutmeg
½ tsp. salt
Optional: 1—2 Tbsp. gluten flour

Mix the wet ingredients together thoroughly. In a separate bowl mix the dry ingredients together. May be sifted. Add the dry mixture to the wet and beat 100—200 strokes. Then add the nuts and mix them in. Lightly oil and flour the pan(s) and scoop the thick mixture into the pan(s). Bake at 350° for 50—60 minutes until golden brown.

Cool the cake before removing from pan(s) and frosting. Frost with cream cheese frosting.

Cream Cheese Frosting
16 oz. cream cheese
½—1 cup honey or add honey to taste
2 tsp. vanilla
Optional: coconut—to sprinkle on top

Leave the cream cheese at room temperature for 1—2 hours until very soft. When the cake is done and cooling, the cream cheese should be soft enough to whip. Use a mixer and slowly mix the honey and vanilla into the cream cheese until smooth. Chill the frosting for an hour or so and then frost the cake. Sprinkle coconut on top if desired.

Dessert Pie Crusts

Add 1 tsp. honey to any of the following recipes if they are to be used for dessert recipes. These recipes may be used for Quiche without the added honey.

Double Pie Crust Recipe
(Makes 1—10″ double crust)

2 cups sifted w.w. flour (at least half pastry flour)
1 tsp. salt
⅔ cup light oil
¼ cup cold milk or cold water
1—2 tsp. liquid lecithin

Mix the wet and dry ingredients separately. Add the dry ingredients to the wet and use a fork or pastry blender to mix. Knead the dough for a couple of minutes and divide it into 2 parts. Roll one part between 2 pieces of wax paper. Roll the dough until it is about ⅛ inch thick and 11—12 inches in diameter. While rolling out the dough be careful to turn it upside down once in a while and lift the wax paper on each side occasionally so it will not stick permanently to the dough. Lightly oil the 10″ pie pan. Remove one layer of wax paper from the rolled dough and turn it upside down over the pie pan. Gently remove the top, last layer of wax paper and shape the pie crust to the pan. Push the dough into the corners of the pan; do not stretch the dough or it will shrink and grow smaller while the pie is baking. Use a fork to poke air holes in the dough.

After shaping the bottom crust, fill it with pie filling and cover it with the second rolled-out pie crust. Flute the edges together, make a few slits on the top crust, and then bake at 425° or 30—40 minutes until golden and flaky. Serve pie hot or chilled.

Single Pie Crust #1
(Makes 2 single crusts)

2 cups sifted w.w. flour (at least half pastry flour)
1 stick butter or margarine—softened but not melted
¼ cup cold water
1–2 tsp. lecithin—liquid
1 tsp. salt

Single Pie Crust #2
(Makes 2 single crusts)

2 cups sifted w.w. flour (at least half pastry flour), or 1¼ cups millet
　　flour and ¾ cup rice flour
½ stick butter or margarine—softened but not melted
¼ cup oil
¼ cup cold water
1–2 tsp. lecithin—liquid
1 tsp. salt

Add the mixed flour and salt to the butter and lecithin and mix as
well as possible. Add the water and continue mixing. Knead a few
minutes and continue making the dough the same as the double
crust recipe except use 2 pie pans and make 2 single crusts. Also bake
the crust 3–5 minutes at 325° *before* adding the filling and then
bake it all together according to the filling recipe. Use this for pies or
quiche.
Note: Crusts made with butter or margarine tend to shrink a little
more, so be careful not to *stretch* the dough.

Pumpkin for Recipes

There are several ways to prepare pumpkin for use in recipes. A
small pumpkin can be boiled whole then seeded and peeled before
mashing and draining off the excess liquid *or* a large pumpkin can be
cut into large pieces, seeded and baked till tender before peeling and

mashing it. (Bake pumpkin about 375° to 400°F for 45–70 minutes.) Canned pumpkin may be used although it is not as fresh or nutritious.

*Some kinds of orange winter squash may be substituted for pumpkin.

Pumpkin Pudding

Blend:
2 cups cooked pumpkin (see recipe)
1–1¼ cups nut milk
⅓–⅔ cup honey *or* maple syrup
2 large eggs
2 Tbsp. arrowroot powder
1 Tbsp. instant milk powder (may be omitted)
2 tsp. vanilla extract
½–1 tsp. cinnamon
¼ tsp. ginger
Several dashes nutmeg and sea salt
Optional: 1 Tbsp. molasses

Blend all ingredients and taste the mixture. Make any changes according to taste. The mixture will be somewhat thick, but very pourable. Lightly oil 1–2 baking dishes and pour the mixture into them about 1½ to 2 inches thick. Bake the pudding at 325°F for about 30 to 45 minutes until the mixture becomes firm and turns golden brown. Chill thoroughly before serving.

Pumpkin Pie

Use a pie crust of your choice. Use the *Pumpkin Pudding* recipe as the filling and bake the same way. One pudding recipe makes 2 to 3 pies. Each piece of pie may be sprinkled with extra cinnamon.

Apple Pie
(1 medium or large pie)

6–8 large baking apples, cored and chopped (peeled, if desired)
½–¾ cup honey *or* ⅓–½ cup maple syrup
2½ Tbsp. arrowroot powder
1½ to 2 tsp. cinnamon
¼ tsp. sea salt
Optional: ½ cup raisins or currants or chopped nuts

Use Rome, Spartan, MacIntosh, Jonathan, Newton, Lodi or other baking apples. Simmer the apples and raisins or currants with ¼ cup water on medium heat for 8 to 10 minutes or until tender. Drain the apples and save the liquid. When the liquid cools, mix it with the arrowroot powder and sea salt. Add 1–2 Tbsp. extra water if needed. Heat it in a saucepan until it thickens, stirring constantly.

Mix the apples, arrowroot mixture and the remaining ingredients together and scoop into 2 pie custs. 1 or 2 Tbsp. of ground nuts may be sprinkled on top for extra flavour and attractiveness.

Bake at 375°F for 25 to 40 minutes, until browned and set. (The larger and thicker the pie, the longer the baking time.)

Pumpkin Cookies
(makes 4–6 dozen)

Dry Ingredients: Sift together
2 cups whole wheat, millet flour or rice flour
½ cup soy, buckwheat, amaranth or whole wheat pastry flour
3 tsp. baking powder
2 tsp. cinnamon
½ tsp. sea salt
½ tsp. nutmeg
¼ tsp. ginger
Optional: 1–2 cups raisins or currants
          1 cup chopped nuts

Wet Ingredients:
½ cup oil (or soft clarified butter)
1–1¼ cup honey *or* ¾ cup maple syrup and ⅓ cup pumpkin liquid
    or water
¾ cup brown date sugar *or* barley malt powder
2 eggs beaten
1 Tbsp. molasses
Optional: 1–2 tsp. vanilla extract

Add: 1½ cups pumpkin (cooked & mashed)

Stir the dry ingredients into the wet. This makes a thick but pourable batter. Bake medium sized cookies for 12–14 minutes at 400°–425°.

Tapioca Treats
(Wheat-free)
(makes 1½ dozen)

¼ cup tapioca flour
¼ cup brown rice flour*
¼ cup barley malt powder*
½ cup crispy brown rice*
½ cup dried, unsweetened coconut* (fine grated)
3 Tbsp. maple syrup
1 tsp. pure vanilla extract

Mix the flours and malt powder together well. Add the maple syrup and vanilla extract and mix thoroughly. Carefully stir in the crispy brown rice, then lastly, mix in the coconut. Shape a teaspoonful of the mixture into a ball and flatten it to about ⅜ inch thick on a lightly oiled cookie sheet. Bake at 350°F for 8–10 minutes. Remove from the oven while they are still soft, but lightly browned. They will harden as they cool. Once cooled (approx. ½ hour), store in a tin with a small crust of bread inside to keep the cookies moist and absorb excess moisture.

*Variations: These may slightly alter the flavour, but not the consistency of the recipe.
*Instead of: Use:
rice flour   millet flour
coconut   ground nuts or seeds
crispy rice   chopped nuts
barley malt   *fine* brown date
sugar (can be ground in blender or food processor or grinder)

Oatmeal Cookies
(Makes 4–5 dozen)

Mix well together:
⅔ cup brown date sugar
½ cup (1 stick) butter or margarine—softened
½ cup honey or ⅜ cup honey and ⅛ cup molasses

Add:
2 cups rolled oats
1 cup w.w. flour
½ cup pastry or unbleached white flour
2 eggs—beaten
1 tsp. cinnamon
1 tsp. vanilla
½ tsp. baking powder (no-alum)
¼ tsp. salt
Few dashes nutmeg

Mix the dry ingredients separately and gradually add them to the wet ingredients.
Make sure the batter is fairly stiff and hard to stir. Add a bit more honey or flour if needed. Drop a spoonful or two of batter per cookie on an oiled cookie sheet. Make sure the cookies are one inch or more apart. Bake for 10–14 minutes or until lightly browned (but tender) at 400°.

Carob Chip-Nut Cookies
(Makes about 4–5 dozen)

Mix well together:
2/3 cup honey
1/2 cup butter or margarine—softened
1/2 cup brown date sugar
1/4 cup milk powder—non-instant
1 egg—beaten
2 tsp. gluten flour or arrowroot powder
1 tsp. vanilla
1/4 tsp. salt

Add and mix in well:
1 cup w.w. flour
3/4 cup carob chips (purchase at health food store)
1/2 cup w.w. pastry or unbleached white flour
1/2 cup chopped walnuts, pecans, or almonds

Drop a spoonful or two of batter for each cookie on a lightly oiled cookie sheet. Bake for 1–12 minutes or till very lightly browned at 375°. These cookies can also be made into *bar cookies* by spreading the batter about 1/2 inch thick on a cookie sheet and baking at 350° for 15–20 minutes. Then cool a few minutes and cut into squares or bars.

Rice Pudding
2 cups pre-cooked brown rice, cold (about 1 cup dry)
1/2 cup milk, nut milk or sweet juice (apple, pear or peach are best)
1/2 cup honey *or* 1/3 cup maple syrup plus 2 Tbsp. extra juice or milk
2 large eggs—beaten foamy
2 tsp. vanilla extract
1–1½ tsp. cinnamon
1/8 tsp. sea salt
Optional: 1/2 cup raisins or currants

Plain, leftover rice may be used or sweet, brown rice, if it is available. Mix all the ingredients together and pour them into a lightly oiled casserole pan about 9"×9" and bake 35–45 minutes uncovered at 375° until 'set' and somewhat firm. Served hot or cold, this makes a delicious easy and nutritious dessert.

Date Squares
(Makes 1 9"×9" Pan)

1 CRUNCHY CRUST RECIPE
1 DATE SPREAD RECIPE

Press ½ or more of the crust recipe onto the bottom only of a lightly oiled 9"×9" pan. Next, spread all the date mixture on. Lastly, evenly 'sprinkle' the remaining crust mixture over the top of the dates and pat them together gently as a top crust. Bake around 350° for 25 to 40 minutes until the top is lightly browned, but still tender. The crust will harden as it cools, don't let it harden in the oven or it will be *very* hard! Cut it into pieces before it cools completely or it will be difficult to cut. A rich dessert or snack!

Date Spread
1 to 11/6 lb. dates—pitted (up to 500 gms)
⅔ cup water
Few dashes salt
Optional: 2 Tbsp. lemon juice, fresh
         1–2 Tbsp. lemon rind—grated fine

Put all ingredients in a saucepan and cook on a low heat to medium-low heat until the dates get soft and mix easily with the water. (About 30 minutes or more.) When the date mixture can be stirred into a pastelike texture, take it off the heat and let it cool before using for Date Squares.

Crunchy Crust
(For Date Squares or Apple Crisp)

Mix:
¾–1 cup honey *or* ⅔ cup maple syrup
½ cup oil
¾ tsp. sea salt

Mix Separately:
2½ cups rolled oats
1 cup whole wheat or oat flour
Optional: 2 Tbsp. lemon rind—grated fine

Slowly add the dry ingredients to the wet and mix well. Use for Date Squares or as a crust for other recipes.

PART IV

STRESS AND DIGESTION

"I learned this, at least, by my experiment;
that if one advances confidently in the
direction of his dreams, and endeavours to
live the life which he has imagined, he will
meet with a success unexpected in common hours."

Thoreau-Walden

CHAPTER 11

Fright to Fight or Flight

We have come a long way in our trip through the body and we can see how disease has a connection, direct or indirect, to sluggish or inefficient digestion. Yet we still have more to learn about digestion. Our trip has started at the mouth and gone down through the muscles of the stomach and intestine, into the blood to the liver and gallbladder, throughout the main bloodstream to the lymphatics and the immune system. To understand how this group of systems and organs works together as a unit we have to leave the microscope and stand back a bit. The parts that we have explored, together form the central core of the body, and they get their nerve energy primarily from the parasympathetic nervous system.

There is another part of the body that is energized primarily by a different nervous system. This is the skeletal muscle system, which gets its nerve energy from the sympathetic nervous system. While the stomach juices are the "spark" for proper digestion, the "sparkplugs" of the sympathetic nervous system are the adrenal glands. The adrenals normally secrete hormones which help maintain mineral and sugar levels. In emergencies, however, they secrete a powerful hormone called adrenalin or epinepherine which shunts energy away from the parasympathetic nervous system (digestive and lymphatic systems), and sends it outwards via the sympathetic nervous system to the skeletal muscles so that you can fight or flee from danger. Obviously, this is called the fight or flight response.

To see how it works in action, picture a zebra out in an open grass-land. He can see that there is no danger in the vicinity, so his main energy is concentrated in the central core of his body. The parasym-pathetic nervous system is dominant, so the digestive and lymph systems are fully activated. He is chewing and the grass goes down into the stomach, which makes digestive juices that stimulate the in-testinal tract. In the intestine, the friendly bacteria are busy baking little grass pies. In the lymph system, the thymus gland is orche-strating the white blood cells which quickly deal with any viruses, yeast, fungi, bacteria, parasites or abnormal cells. The skeletal mus-cles of the legs are used at the moment for little more than props.

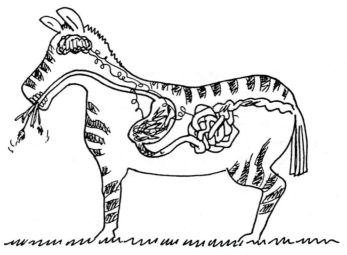

Now picture that same zebra with a massive lion barreling through the tall grass directly towards the zebra, drool pouring from his jaws and a hungry glint in his eyes. Does this zebra care whether there's a little undigested grass in his intestine? Does he care if there's a virus or two hiding out somewhere in the lymph system? Emphatically, NO! Forget about those trivialities, let's get these legs moving, fast! So the adrenal glands fire up, and the energy switches from the central core of the body to the skeletal muscles, and the ze·bra either kicks the lion in the chops or "hightails" it out of there.

Within minutes, it's almost all over one way or the other. Either the zebra made good his getaway, or he's become dinner for Leo and

friends. If he got away, within a short time the adrenal glands would stop making fight or flight hormones. The adrenal hormones in the blood would be broken down and the energy would slowly shift away from the skeletal muscles and back to the digestive and lymph system. Within a short time he would be back to grazing. Even if the lion was still within sight, as long as he was outside the zebra's "safety zone", the zebra would continue peacefully grazing.

Real physical danger is a rarity in our society. The wild beasts have long since been exterminated from populated areas or locked up in zoos.

However, we have a built-in video screen in our minds on which we are constantly projecting pictures. This has great uses for we can take experiences from the past and present and then project them into the future on our mental screen. From this information we can then anticipate what problems and/or opportunities might arise in the future so that we can best prepare for them.

The problem is that when you project a picture of a potential problem in your mind your body doesn't know that it is not a real problem, that it is merely an imaginary potential problem. The body reacts exactly as if you were in extreme physical danger. The body energy shifts away from the digestive organs and lymph system and out to the skeletal muscles so that you can run from or fight with

this "roaring lion" of the mind. In nature a real situation like this would usually be resolved within minutes. However, our minds have the incredible ability to create more and more and more potential problems.

We spend a great deal of time trying to avoid these problem pictures. We can temporarily obliberate them by using drugs and alcohol. We can avoid them briefly by taking holidays, going fishing, playing cards, sports or other games, watching t.v., sleeping in, being too busy, etc., but often as soon as we stop these activities the mind begins to fill again with all the potential troubles that might occur.

Outside sources often contribute to a sense of danger and trouble. Newspapers and T.V. news exaggerates the amount of real danger that exists in our communities.

Also we even pride ourselves when we use our minds to our best advantage. If we use our mind to see a situation sooner or clearer than someone else so that we can make a quicker or better deal, then this is something that we boast or brag about. There is, however, a very fine line between practical use of the mind's creative abilities and using it as a scheming machine.

Even a small real problem can turn into a major health problem by constantly thinking about it rather than doing something constructive to resolve it. Problems should be quickly and decisively dealt with or, if they can't be dealt with summarily, they should be consciously put aside until they can be dealt with.

Talking about a problem with a good friend or a counsellor may help to shrink it back to its proper size after a runaway mind has exaggerated it out of proportion.

Since during stress the body is shunting energy into the skeletal muscle system for fight or flight why not follow through with some vigorous exercise. Running, aerobics, cycling, martial arts, swimming, etc., are good ways to burn up accumulated stress and help remove the sense of powerlessness that often accompanies it.

There are softer forms such as tai-chi and yoga, relaxation classes, meditation and breathing excercises that can help rebalance the mind and body.

Water therapy can be very effective at de-stressing. Since the skin is the major sense organ of the body, immersing it in water can give a sense of nurture. Water temperature above body temperature is relaxing for a short period of time. Excess heat can be weakening however so heat is best followed by cold.

There is a simple technique that can be used to disengage the mental activity from having a negative impact on the body. You touch three fingers from each hand on the corners of the forehead and then pull the skin lightly apart so the skin in the center of the forehead is slightly stretched. With muscle testing it has been found that if you now think about a particular problem it won't weaken the body. Holding these points seems to work as a clutch to effectively disengage the mental activity from the physical body. If these points are held for a few minutes it takes the "sharper edges" off the problem for hours.

If having a "bad" picture in the mind has a bad effect on the body, even if the picture is not real, then a good picture in the mind should have a good effect on the body, even if it's not real. This has proven true in many clinical studies. Children with cancer play a game like Pac-Man but on the screen it uses white blood cells chasing cancers cells. The result is increased activity of their own white blood cells.

Creative visualization is a rapidly growing form of therapy and can be done easily. Sit or lie down in a comfortable position. You can start by thinking about a particular problem. However you have unlimited tools available. You can visualize anything from a machine gun and hand grenades to a magic wand and fairy dust to change the picture on your mind's video screen from that of a problem into one with a happy ending. If you create an improved picture in your mind your subconscious will immediately swing all its powers into having that picture expressed into physical reality. Jules Vernes imagined undersea travel and that made the submarine virtually inevitable.

Positive thinking is a form of creative visualization. If what comes out of our mouth is indicative of what goes on in our minds then let us speak words of support and encouragement. This is especially important with young children as they are forming much of their self image from feedback from those around them. Everything seen and heard is recorded as reality so until the ability to discriminate is learned it's especially important to avoid continually berating a child.

PRICELESS PEACE OF MIND

There may be a point where everything we do becomes futile and pointless. The more we struggle the more mired we become. This is the point where surrender may be more beneficial than furthur struggle.

There is a certain wisdom behind peasant philosophy. What is beyond your control is simply shrugged off. "C'est la vie", "That's life" indicate surrender to greater forces. However, the point where you should fight and where you should flee is not always easy to know.

> "God grant me the serenity to accept
> the things I cannot change,
> courage to change the things I can
> and wisdom to know the difference."
>   Anonymous

While physical pain and disease are messages from your body that something's wrong and change is necessary, despair is God's message that something is not right spiritually. We take joy and pride when we mentally and physically force our way through life's problems. Depression and despair, however, are the rewards for our failures. We get so caught up in our little skirmishes that we often miss the bigger picture.

If we lay back on the grass on a clear summer night we can see what appears to be endless numbers of twinkling stars. The universe seems immense. Actually you can only see a few thousand stars with the naked eye, but it is now known that there are over two hundred billion stars in our galaxy, the Milky Way. Also, there are approximately one hundred billion known galaxies.

Our life's dramas of victory and defeat begin to pale in comparison with the gigantic stage on which they are being played out.

With such immensity it would seem that our lives must be lonely and insignificant.

"One night a man had a dream. He dreamed he was walking along the beach with the LORD. Across the sky flashed scenes from his life. For each scene, he noticed two sets of footprints in the sand; one belonging to him, and the other to the LORD.

When the last scene of his life flashed before him, he looked back at the footprints in the sand. He noticed that many times along the path of his life there was only one set of footprint. He also noticed that it happened at the very lowest and saddest times in his life. This really bothered him and he questioned the LORD about it. "LORD, you said that once I decided to follow you, you'd walk with me all the way. But I have noticed that during the most troublesome times in my life, there is

only one set of footprints. I don't
understand why when I needed you
most you would leave me."
The LORD replied, "My precious,
precious child, I love you and I would
never leave you. During your times of
trial and suffering, when you see only
one set of footprints, it was then that I
carried you."

Anonymous

We worry and struggle because we feel alone in life and our alone-
ness makes us fearful. All of this weakens us however and it is not
what God intended for us.

"I came that they might have life, and
might have it abundantly." (John 10:10)

Could the promise of abundant life apply to every little lost soul in
this vast universe?

"Behold, I stand at the door and knock;
if any one hears My voice and opens the door,
I will come in to him." (Revelation 3:20)

How do you open the door to God? By prayer. Do you need a degree or a course to pray or authorization from someone else? No, all
you need is desire. Here is a sample prayer titled "The Difficulties of
Praying."

" Why, O Lord, is it so hard for me to keep my heart
directed toward you? Why do the many little things I
want to do, and the many people I know, keep crowding
into my mind, even during the hours that I am totally free
to be with you and you alone? Why does my mind
wander off in so many directions, and why does my heart
desire the things that lead me astray? Are you not enough
for me? Do I keep doubting your love and care, your

mercy and grace? Do I keep wondering, in the centre of my being, whether you will give me all I need if I just keep my eyes on you?

Please accept my distractions, my fatigue, my irritations, and my faithless wanderings. You know me more deeply and fully than I know myself. You love me with a greater love than I can love myself. You can offer me more than I can desire. Look at me, see me in all my misery and inner confusion, and let me sense your presence in the midst of my turmoil. All I can do is show myself to you. Yet, I am afraid to do so. I am afraid that you will reject me. But, I know-with the knowledge of faith-that you desire to give me your love. The only thing you ask of me is not to hide from you, not to run away in despair, not to act as if you were a relentless despot.

Take my tired body, my confused mind, and my restless soul into your arms and give me rest, simple quiet rest. So I ask too much too soon? I should not worry about that. You will let me know. Come, Lord, come. Amen."

(Author Unknown)

INDEX

To find a Naturopathic Physician in your area,
please contact:

Association of Naturopathic Physicians
of British Columbia
Suite #204 - 2786 West 16th Avenue
Vancouver, British Columbia V6K 3C4
(604) 732-7070   Fax: (604) 732-3709

or

Ontario Naturopathic Association
at Ontario College of Naturopathic Medicine
60 Berl Avenue
Toronto, Ontario M8Y 3C7
(416) 251-5261   Fax: (416) 251-5883

or

American Association
of Naturopathic Physicians
P.O. Box 20386
Seattle, Washington 98102
(206) 323-7610

or

Standard Process Labs, Inc.
Milwaukee, Wisconsin
U.S.A.
(414) 495-2122

NOTES

Guidesheets to the Three Stages of Eating Alive

When using the following charts remember:

To regain stomach function: No White Sugar, Coffee, Tea, Chocolate, Alcohol, Yeast, or any other know sensitivities.

To make surplus digestive juice, go light in morning.

To help intestine, avoid refined foods, and avoid coarse, scratchy fiber.

To speed up digestion, follow the above food combinations as much as possible.

To slow down critter digestion, take *lactobacilli acidophilus* bacteria capsules 1-2, twice a day. Also garlic.

Take yeast killers as directed.

To speed up lymph drainage, rub chest and legs daily with shower brush or loofa sponge. Also exercise.

Solve your problems, or surrender them, don't dwell on them!

Note: Sweets don't mix with proteins for anyone. Acids don't mix with starches for many people.

Suggestion: For convenience you may wish to remove the ''Guidesheets'' from the book to keep them handy in your kitchen where they will be available for a quick review, or, when you are planning your weekly menus.

DON'T MIX

STAGE I   3 weeks

positive	neutral	negative
Acid Fruits 7–11a.m. 1 hr. digestion recipe— 1 cup hot water with 2 Tbsp. lemon juice (or juice of ½ lemon) pinch of cayenne (and, or, ginger) pure maple syrup (to taste, optional) grapefruit (fresh) grapefruit (cooked) apple cider vinegar - *Building Foods* protein Vegetable Protein 3–4 hr. dig. rice polishings soya bean soya flour tofu Raw Nuts— almonds coconuts cashews Brazil nuts filberts walnuts etc. Animal Protein 3–4 hr. dg. Dairy Protein (not yet) Flesh Protein 4–6 hr. dg. Fish— bass cod crab halibut oysters salmon shrimp sole tuna Lean Meats— beef liver (calves) chicken turkey lamb veal wild game	*Protective Foods* can be used with either positive or negative Non-Starchy Vegetables avocado beans (green & wax) beets & beet tops broccoli Brussel sprouts cabbage carrots cauliflour celery chives cucumber dandelion egg plant endive escarole garlic kale kohlrabí leek mustard greens nettles okra onion parsley peas peppers (green & red) radishes romaine rutabagas salsify (oyster plant) spinach Swiss chard sprouts turnips (white & yellow) watercress zucchini herbs Fats & Oils use sparingly cream butter margarine (unhydrogenated) safflower oil sunflower oil flax seed oil (uncooked & fresh) - *Water* is the most neutral food & can be consumed any time except while actually *eating*. Spring water is preferred.	*Energy Foods* carbohydrate Starches 2–3 hr. digestion Grains— barley brown rice buckwheat corn (dried) flax oats & oat bran rye millet sesame Starchy Vegetables— beans (dry) corn lentils peas (dry) parsnip potatoes (& yams, & sweet) pumpkin squash Jerusalem artichoke Fruit 1 hr. digestion best in season Sub-Acid Fruits— apples apricots black currants blackberries blueberries cherries grapes huckleberries mangos peaches pears plums raspberries strawberries To Be Eaten Alone— oranges canteloupe melons watermelon Enzyme Fruits— papaya (raw) pineapple (raw) kiwi - Sweet Fruits— bananas dates figs raisins currants very ripe fruit *Natural Sweets* Blackstrap molasses carob honey (unpasturized) maple syrup maple sugar raw sugar

DON'T MIX

STAGE II   4 weeks

positive	neutral	negative

Acid Fruits
7–11a.m. 1 hr. digestion
recipe—
1 cup hot water with
2 Tbsp. lemon juice (or
  juice of ½ lemon)
  pinch of cayenne (and,
  or, ginger) pure maple
  syrup (to taste,
  optional)
 	
grapefruit (fresh)
grapefruit (cooked)
apple cider vinegar
tomatoes (cooked)
cranberries
rhubarb
- - - - - - - - - - - - - - - - -
Building Foods protein
Vegetable Protein
3–4 hr. dig.
  rice polishings
  soya bean
  soya flour
  tofu
Raw Nuts—
  almonds
  coconuts
  cashews
  Brazil nuts
  filberts
  walnuts
  peanuts
  etc.
Animal Protein
3–4 hr. dig.
  eggs
Dairy
  acidophilus milk
  buttermilk
  cheese
  yogurt
Flesh Protein 4–6 hr. dg.
Fish—
  bass
  cod
  crab
  halibut
  oysters
  salmon
  shrimp
  sole
  tuna
Lean Meats—
  beef
  liver (calves)
  chicken
  turkey
  lamb
  veal
  wild game
  pork
	Protective Foods
	can be used with either
	positive or negative
	Non-Starchy Vegetables
	  avocado
	  beans (green & wax)
	  beets & beet tops
	  broccoli
	  Brussel sprouts
	  cabbage
	  carrots
	  cauliflour
	  celery
	  chives
	  cucumber
	  dandelion
	  egg plant
	  endive
	  escarole
	  garlic
	  kale
	  kohlrabi
	  leek
	  mustard greens
	  nettles
	  okra
	  onion
	  parsley
	  peas
	  peppers (green & red)
	  radishes
	  romaine (lettuce)
	  rutabagas
	  salsify (oyster plant)
	  spinach
	  Swiss chard
	  sprouts
	  turnips (white &
	    yellow)
	  watercress
	  zucchini
	  herbs
	  asparagus
	  mushrooms
	  tomatoes (raw)
	Fats & Oils use sparingly
	  cream
	  butter
	  margarine
	    (unhydrogenated)
	  safflower oil
	  sunflower oil
	  flax seed oil (uncooked
	    & fresh)
	- - - - - - - - - - - - - - - - - - -
	Water is the most neutral
	food & can be consumed
	any time except while
	actually *eating.*
	
	Spring water is preferred.
		Energy Foods
		carbohydrate Starches
		2–3 hr. digestion
		Grains—
		  barley
		  brown rice
		  buckwheat
		  corn (dried)
		  flax
		  oats & oat bran
		  rye
		  millet
		  sesame
		  wheat
		Starchy Vegetables—
		  beans (dry)
		  corn
		  lentils
		  peas (dry)
		  parsnip
		  potatoes (& yams, &
		    sweet)
		  pumpkin
		  squash
		  Jerusalem artichoke
		
		Fruit 1 hr. digestion best
		in season
		Sub-Acid Fruits—
		  apples
		  apricots
		  black currants
		  blackberries
		  blueberries
		  cherries
		  grapes
		  huckleberries
		  mangos
		  peaches
		  pears
		  plums
		  raspberries
		  strawberries
		
		To Be Eaten Alone—
		  oranges
		  canteloupe
		  melons
		  watermelon
		
		Enzyme Fruits—
		  papaya (raw)
		  pineapple (raw)
		  kiwi
		- - - - - - - - - - - - - - - - - - -
		Sweet Fruits—
		  bananas
		  dates
		  figs
		  raisins
		  currants
		  very ripe fruit
		Natural Sweets
		  Blackstrap molasses
		  carob
		  honey (unpasturized)
		  maple syrup
		  maple sugar
		  raw sugar

DON'T MIX

STAGE III

positive	neutral	negative

Acid Fruits
7–11a.m. 1 hr. digestion
recipe—
1 cup hot water with
2 Tbsp. lemon juice (or
  juice of ½ lemon)
  pinch of cayenne (and,
  or, ginger) pure maple
  syrup (to taste,
  optional)
——
grapefruit (fresh)
grapefruit (cooked)
apple cider vinegar
tomatoes (cooked)
cranberries
rhubarb
	Protective Foods
	can be used with either
	positive or negative
	Non-Starchy Vegetables
	  avocado
	  beans (green & wax)
	  beets & beet tops
	  broccoli
	  Brussel sprouts
	  cabbage
	  carrots
	  cauliflour
	  celery
	  chives
	  cucumber
	  dandelion
	  egg plant
	  endive
		Energy Foods
		carbohydrate Starches
		2–3 hr. digestion
		Grains—
		  barley
		  brown rice
		  buckwheat
		  corn (dried)
		  flax
		  oats & oat bran
		  rye
		  millet
		  sesame
		  wheat
		Starchy Vegetables—
		  beans (dry)
		  corn
		  lentils

Building Foods protein
Vegetable Protein
3–4 hr. dig.
  rice polishings
  soya bean
  soya flour
  tofu
Raw Nuts—
  almonds
  coconuts
  cashews
  Brazil nuts
  filberts
  walnuts
  peanuts
Animal Protein
3–4 hr. dig.
  eggs
 	
Dairy
  acidophilus milk
  buttermilk
  cheese
  yogurt
Flesh Protein 4–6 hr. dg.
Fish—
  bass
  cod
  crab
  halibut
  oysters
  salmon
  shrimp
  sole
  tuna
Lean Meats—
  beef
  liver (calves)
  chicken
  turkey
  lamb
  veal
  wild game
  pork
	escarole
	  garlic
	  kale
	  kohlrabi
	  leek
	  mustard greens
	  nettles
	  okra
	  onion
	  parsley
	  peas
	  peppers (green & red)
	  radishes
	  romaine (lettuce)
	  rutabagas
	  salsify (oyster plant)
	  spinach
	  Swiss chard
	  sprouts
	  turnips (white &
	    yellow)
	  watercress
	  zucchini
	  herbs
	  asparagus
	  mushrooms
	  tomatoes (raw)
	Fats & Oils use sparingly
	  cream
	  butter
	  margarine
	    (unhydrogenated)
	  safflower oil
	  sunflower oil
	  flax seed oil (uncooked
	    & fresh)
	
	Water is the most neutral
	food & can be consumed
	any time except while
	actually *eating*.
	
	Spring water is preferred.
		peas (dry)
		  parsnip
		  potatoes (& yams, &
		    sweet)
		  pumpkin
		  squash
		  Jerusalem artichoke
		————
		Fruit 1 hr. digestion best
		in season
		
		Sub-Acid Fruits—
		  apples
		  apricots
		  black currants
		  blackberries
		  blueberries
		  cherries
		  grapes
		  huckleberries
		  mangos
		  peaches
		  pears
		  plums
		  raspberries
		  strawberries
		
		  oranges
		  canteloupe
		  melons
		  watermelon
		
		Enzyme Fruits—
		  papaya (raw)
		  pineapple (raw)
		  kiwi
		Sweet Fruits—
		  bananas
		  dates
		  figs
		  raisins
		  currants
		  very ripe fruit
		Natural Sweets
		  Blackstrap molasses
		  carob
		  honey (unpasturized)
		  maple syrup
		  maple sugar
		  raw sugar